# Why Daughters Need Their Dads

ALSO BY K.T. RIGHTER

*The Tao Te Ching De-Coded*


Contact the author at: kt123trailblazer@gmail.com

KETNA Publishing
PO Box 90861 Burton, Michigan 48509

# Why Daughters Need Their Dads

## The Powerful Secrets That Will Help Any Woman Finally Reach Her Dreams

**K.T. Righter**

KETNA Publishing
P.O Box 90861 Burton, Michigan 48509

Copyright © 2015 by Kevin Thomas

All rights reserved, including the right to reproduce this book or portions thereof in any form whatsoever.

For information, address KETNA Publishing
P.O Box 90861 Burton, Michigan 48509

First KETNA Printing Edition 2015

Cover Design by Erik Naugle
Book design by Maureen Cutajar

 is a registered trademark of KETNA Publishing.

Printed in the USA

Library of Congress Control Number: 2015907395

ISBN: 978-0-9963874-1-5 (Softcover)

# DEDICATION

This book is dedicated to you. God has brought us together for a reason; I really believe that. The reasons can be many, including understanding how a daughter creates the life she wants and deserves by understanding her dad and if you are a dad, to help further understand your daughter to guide her to be successful and happy in life. Whatever the reason, this book can change your life. It is also dedicated to my three daughters: Caroline, Kimberly, and Cheyenne. They are the initial reason I wrote this book. It began as a love letter and guide to help them create the love and lives they desire, and now my hope is that it becomes the same for you. May love and peace guide you in your journey and may God be with you.

# ACKNOWLEDGEMENTS

You might think that an acknowledgment would not be an important part of any book, let alone this book. However, this book is different. The truth is, the very reason I am writing this book is because of what God has done for me.

"Oh sure," you say. "Many people thank God for this or that." However, it isn't or wasn't that easy for me. I've always believed in God—always felt him watching out for me. Yet I never let him take control of my life until the last several years. As you might have guessed, this created problems for me before this time—a lot of problems. I went through times of severe testing and times when people questioned everything about me. I wasn't perfect and I made mistakes, but I knew some things that were said were greatly exaggerated, half-truths, or outright lies. This would have destroyed some people. For me, however, it only challenged my survival instincts and that's what I became: a survivor. Not only that, but I became happier as days went by and more determined to make the most of life. It also took time, but I learned from my mistakes and I learned to forgive—to dig deep and really forgive both others and myself. Eventually, I actually saw these challenges as a gift because I was lucky enough to find out who my real friends were when things weren't going my way.

At first, it wasn't easy. I would pray and often nothing happened. The reason was simple: I was going to do it my way no matter what, much to my detriment. All the while I thought I was smarter than God or perhaps wanted to live life as I wanted and thought I was "helping" him. Funny thing about God is that he doesn't need anyone's help; he knows what he is doing. At times when frustration came, I would slip back to ways that were not healthy. I was stubborn enough that this reoccurred for years. I put on a good show, was happy-go-lucky, and full of smiles, but sometimes that smile masked the pain. Until…the light bulb finally went on. I hit my personal rock bottom and made a simple decision: I could live or I could die. Basically, I chose to live and more importantly, to live for God. I chose to put bad times, bad choices, bad relationships, and for the most part, bad habits, behind me.

Again, I was not perfect. But like everyone else, I was striving to be. I made mistakes, but this time, things were different. I really did let God take control and he finally revealed himself to me because I let him take the wheel of my life. Things started to happen and I was on my way.

After that, it got easier. Instead of praying or asking God for something knowing full well I was going to do what I wanted in the end, I actually put my life in his hands, realizing he would only reveal himself to those who really believe and obey. That was the key.

I was now in my mid-forties and I started to follow dreams He wanted for me. By letting go, I began to gain. I went back to school, won academic awards, went into the medical field, did some sports writing, appeared in newspapers, wrote some books, and most importantly, my spiritual life was back on track. Jesus and I developed a nice relationship. I would lie in bed before I got up and talk to Him. Before bed, I would lay in the dark and talk to Him some more. It also became a lesson in thinking and compassion for me. Things would never be the same again. He gave me the ability to open my eyes and do some free thinking.

Free thinking has helped me enormously along the way and I can thank God for that as well. He gave me the ability to look at things and to have the ability to question things. I remember sitting in a college class one day and the professor showed a picture of two small children. He said the one on the left had learning disabilities and various physical defects. He said the one on the right was a perfectly healthy child. Our job was to look at the pictures and find all the reasons why the child on the left looked sick and all the reasons why this child on the right looked healthy. Students got their pens out and busily scribbled down notes as they studied the pictures. It appeared everyone was writing something down except for me.

Then the professor asked people to volunteer their answers. We went around the room and almost everybody could find reasons to validate the professor: the eyes were a little different, or the nose was different, and so on. Nearly everybody found something different, except me. I sat there thinking that perhaps I wasn't getting it or perhaps I missed something. Now, if you know me, you know that I am not shy about sharing in class. The professor noticed this and, much to my dismay, called upon me.

"Mr. Thomas," he said with a smile, "you haven't said anything."

"Well," I said, "I just don't see it. They don't look that much different to me. In fact, the one on the left looks a hair better than the child on the right to me."

As you can expect, there was some audible laughter and smiles. Some students were trying to explain it to me. They were sure I was dense. The professor moved from behind the podium, slowly walked to the front of the class, and looked directly at me. "Ladies and gentlemen," he said, "Mr. Thomas has been the only one to get this exercise correct."

The professor had given the wrong attributes to each child on purpose to see if we would catch it. The child on the left was actually healthy and the one on the right was sick. That day taught me some valuable lessons. It taught me to trust myself, have compassion for others, and not to judge a book by its cover. It also helped to reinforce my outside the box thinking, so to speak. My friends, besides the research I've included, that's what this book is all about. It's an opportunity for you to come here with an open mind and to think for yourself—to examine all the possibilities that can change your life.

Anyway, let's get to the people I want to thank. First and foremost, I want to thank God and my personal savior, Jesus Christ. Through Them, I found a power I never had before, and realized that I don't have to be perfect, but I can be forgiven.

To my children, Isiah, Caroline, Kimberly, and Cheyenne: three beautiful daughters among them and their very supportive and handsome brother, my son. They are the very inspiration for this book.

To my mother, June and father, Grover: for more support and love than you can imagine. They stuck by me when others doubted me and I can never repay them.

To my brother, Grover: his long-lasting, spiritual journey is a true inspiration compared to the prodigal son path that I ventured on.

To my sister, Debbie: her unconditional love means a lot.

To my youngest brother, John: he is a true example of character and strength.

To my friend, Erik: I have no words for what you have meant to me. Wait, yes I do: you have been a rock as a friend, a great listener, always there when I need you, patient and kind to all, the most intelligent person I have met, and most importantly, a great fishing buddy. You are my third brother.

To Barb: when I thought I was losing everything or overwhelmed by life, you were always there with an inspiration note or kind words and you dug deep to find out who I was and to comfort me. That will never be forgotten.

To all the rest of my family and friends who have provided a source of strength and guidance: I thank you.

To Kelly Bixler of thewriteproofreader.com and her co-editor Sean Burns: Thank you for your editorial assistance in preparing this manuscript for publication.

Finally, this is a book resulting from the inspiration and great wisdom of the great thinkers who have shaped my thoughts over time and I thank all of them as well.

# CONTENTS

| | |
|---|---|
| **INTRODUCTION** | 1 |
| **SECTION ONE: THE RESEARCH** | 7 |
| Overview | 9 |
| Changing the Perception | 10 |
| The Importance of a Father | 11 |
| More Assertive Girls | 12 |
| Emotional Stability | 13 |
| Self-Esteem Through Physical Affection | 14 |
| Nurturing Dads Mean Happy Daughters | 15 |
| Better Sexual Choices | 16 |
| Academic and Job Success Means Earning Power | 17 |
| Live Longer and Prevent Deviant Behavior | 19 |
| Significant Statistics | 21 |
| Father's Prevent Abuse | 23 |
| Better Body Image | 24 |
| Better Grades, Less Drop Outs | 25 |
| Two Parents Are Better Than One | 26 |
| Research Summary | 27 |
| Where Do I Go From Here? | 28 |

**SECTION TWO: THE SOLUTION** ................................................................. 31
The Affection Secret ........................................................................ 33
The Good Role Model Secret ....................................................... 39
The Leadership Secret ..................................................................... 45
The Passion Secret ........................................................................... 53
The Activities Secret ....................................................................... 60
The Communication Secret ......................................................... 65
The Crisis Secret .............................................................................. 74
The Discipline Secret ..................................................................... 85
The Dating Secret ........................................................................... 94
The Handling Sex Secret ............................................................... 103
The Body Image Secret ................................................................. 112
Focus On Her Ideals Secret ......................................................... 121
The Resolve Secret .......................................................................... 131
The Support Secret ........................................................................ 145
The Spiritual Life Secret .............................................................. 154
It's About the Love Secret ............................................................ 164

References ........................................................................................... 171
About the Author ............................................................................. 175

# INTRODUCTION

The true dilemma in life is that we are losing the greatest treasure in the world—our daughters—to an increasing blend of dysfunction and chaos. With each continuing day, a woman will increase her chances of making a bad choice and potentially damaging her life forever. The choices could come from an abundance of things that look enticing: bad drugs, bad men, bad habits, even bad food and drink. Why does this happen? Is it simply as easy as a matter of choice? Actually, it is much deeper than that. Many of the choices that women make today have a secret, unconscious source. A source that is connected deep to her inner soul and often unrealized. A source that is often overlooked: that source is…her own father. Could this really be the key and secret for a daughter to turn her life around? The research on this topic is simply amazing and took my breath away with each journal and reference page I turned. Why did some women seem to have happier and more joyful lives than other women? Why were other women in rocky relationships, hooked on drugs, or lost in depression? Why was some of this information suppressed? Surprisingly, or maybe not surprisingly, the research showed the common denominators for a daughter's successes and failures are her father, their relationship, and the perception of that relationship.

Many times, women don't know why or can't tell you exactly why they make some of the choices they do. A disconnect is made in trying to "figure things out" and blame is tossed around to others and even themselves. The true goal then should be to become aware of what is happening in a woman's life and make adjustments from there, growing one day at a time to become the woman she wants to be. Since women like to communicate, there is usually not a lack of female perspective in a woman's life. However, this is a unique opportunity to embrace a different perspective that I want to share with you and my own daughters on the winding road of this thing called life.

Please allow me to "adopt" you as you read this book—as someone who can help lead you back to reconnecting in your mind, if not in person, with your own father and more importantly, to change your life forever. The fact is, if you want true happiness in life, pursuing this relationship with your father in some form and/or changing your thinking about him is critical to your success and happiness in life.

I really think that the key to our future and of our society is the functionality and social adjustment of our women as changing and more demanding expectations are heaped upon them. Right now, many of them are not handling it well. Depression in women is on the rise, as are other negative factors, especially if there is a dysfunctional relationship with their father. Subconsciously, this does considerable damage to a woman while consciously, she may not even be aware of it. Ask women how they feel today and it is usually met with words like "tired," "fatigued," and "overwhelmed." This is not a good sign, as you can imagine.

The good news is that this book will change your life forever and it was painstakingly put together to ensure your success. Section one covers the research. In section two, 110 "success traits" needed for happiness were organized into 16 categories or "secrets" to prevent redundancy. The reason for this is that some traits overlap, but all individually stand out in one way or another because they are needed for true happiness and success. The goal is to actually apply these key points to your life, not to lose them in a cloud of words. Therefore, each trait is important and will lead you to becoming the woman you want to become and the daughter any father would be proud of.

It is meant to be a book that you can apply to your life, not a book that is full of psycho-babble that leaves you more confused. If there is one thing in this book that leads you to becoming more successful, a better daughter, or even a more understanding father—if just one person is helped by reading this—then this book will be considered a success. As you notice these new changes in your life, embrace this success, as some can be afraid of change, sabotage their progress, and fall back into dysfunction. Don't let this be you. Stay the course. You are not a victim, you are a winner, and I and others need you to be the person you want to be. If you become that, then all of society wins.

# Contract with Myself

I dedicate and commit myself to changing my life for the better.

_____

Your Name

# You Can Make the Difference in the Lives of Others

One day, a man on vacation noticed a young boy trying to save starfish that had washed up in the tide and were certain to die in the hot sun. As quickly as he could, this boy picked up the starfish and threw them back in the ocean.

The man tried to explain the boy's nonsensical ways to him. "I've noticed what you are doing, son, and I know you mean well, but there are millions of starfish all over the world that are dying. You might find something better to do with your time as this will hardly make a difference."

The boy glanced up at the man then looked down at a starfish by his feet. He picked up the beautiful starfish, looked at it for a moment, and then tossed it back into the ocean and said, "It made a difference to that one."

(Paraphrased from the "*Star Thrower*" by Loren Eiseley)

# SECTION ONE
# The Research

## Connecting a Daughter's Success to Her Father

## 1

# OVERVIEW

The influence a father has in the positive development of a daughter has largely been ignored, or its importance not well understood. In these cases, the girls, both younger and older, experience overt symptoms of severe stress when parents divorce and she then lives with her single mother or acquires a stepfather (Amato, Hetherington, & Clingempeel, 1992). This especially happens with adolescent girls who are more likely to be depressed and begin taking drugs. These are just a couple of the many examples we will explore in researching why fathers are critical to the success of their daughters.

In this book, I will outline how daughters react to divorce as well as the many physical, emotional, and academic benefits of an actively involved father. Also, research will be explored regarding problems resulting from an absent father.

## 2

# CHANGING THE PERCEPTION

Clearly, textbooks show an unfavorable bias toward fathers and fail to see the importance in the development of their children, especially with their daughters. Perhaps some people and many mothers do not understand the importance of fathers and the special needs of their daughters that can only be provided by the actively involved father. When girls fail to adjust to divorce in a positive way, instead of stating the obvious breaking of a special bond between a father and daughter as a cause of turmoil and failure to adjust, textbooks will say the cause of turmoil is actually "feeling displaced from a special position in the family system that she held after her parents' divorce and before her mother's remarriage" (Boyd & Bee, 2006). This dangerous thinking then indicates that any male or father figure can come in and replace the previous male figure—that being the biological father—and that the turmoil and stress is not caused by the loss of her father but of a temporary position. This is simply not so or is conjecture at best. It endangers the very success of these girls throughout childhood and into adulthood as we will show in the research. In fact, many displaced fathers have voiced feelings of being pushed out of their children's lives by their former spouse or from a lack of education, and from political agendas of some modern feminists who feel a father is expendable as a parent.

## 3

# THE IMPORTANCE OF A FATHER

From the moment a girl enters this world, research shows the primary reason for her success will be the cause and effect relationship she will have with her father. For instance, from a young age, girls whose fathers are present experience a calming influence which allows them to manage both home stress and school better, get along with others easier, and therefore function better in their daily lives (Pedersen, 1980). Also, those daughters who are in their early formative years of life become more adept at figuring things out in regards to problem solving if the father is present and involved, which develops their self-confidence and self-esteem (Esterbrooks & Golberg, 1984). More amazingly, cognitive and mental development has been shown to be greatly increased for a young girl when their dad is present as opposed to an absentee father. This is especially true if the father is involved in the first six months and increases as the father stays involved (Pedersen, 1980).

Theories abound in terms of the parental bond formed between father and daughter for this happening. Perhaps it's his masculine, reassuring voice and strong hands that come to mean trust, love, care, affection, and reassurance. Certainly his interacting and playing with child in various ways plays a part as well. Regardless, this is significant scientific data.

## 4

# MORE ASSERTIVE GIRLS

Fathers also make a positive impact on their daughters in terms of social interaction during their teenage years. Girls without a father become less assertive and withdrawn instead of becoming more independent and they are less able to handle these situations in a positive manner (Coley, 1998). Assertiveness has an important correlation to self-esteem issues, which plague teenage girls who are bombarded with body issues through magazines, peer pressure, or other sources. These teenage girls are less likely to have eating disorders and body image issues if dad is around.

Some researchers believe that fathers are the first true love of a daughter and that is probably best explained by the overwhelming emotion that fathers feel during marriage ceremonies when giving their daughters away to start a new life. The happiness of the moment can be mixed with emotions of sadness and loss for father and daughter.

## 5

# EMOTIONAL STABILITY

The *American Journal of Preventive Medicine* revealed that daughters who had a sense that their fathers were connected to them and cared about them had far fewer suicide attempts, issues with body dissatisfaction or image, depression, self-esteem issues, drug and alcohol use, and eating disorders. In addition, girls who lived with both parents as opposed to just mothers have fewer development and growth delays, fewer learning disorders, and fewer emotional disabilities and behavior problems (Zill & Schoenborn, 1990).

# 6

# SELF-ESTEEM THROUGH PHYSICAL AFFECTION

Being involved means physical affection as well. Research indicates the best predictor for a daughter's self-esteem is physical touch and physical affection from her father (Duncan, Hill, & Yeung, 1996). In this day and age we live in with abuse accusations prevalent because of contentious divorce, some fathers are afraid to interact in an appropriate manner for fear of being falsely accused. However, few things can be more damaging to a daughter than to withhold affection, whether the father lives in the same household or not. We are touch receptive human beings. Expressing physical affection is a way to express love, care, and acceptance of those we love. It reaffirms her worth as one who is worthy of being, thus raising her self-esteem. It makes her feel loved, comforted, supported, and protected.

# 7

# NURTURING DADS MEAN HAPPY DAUGHTERS

This brings up the issue of bad touch versus good touch. An absentee or non-involved father, whether from divorce or for other reasons, leaves daughters at a much higher risk for sexual abuse from a stepfather, mom's new boyfriend or male coworker, an uncle, male friends of the family, or even other females. Biological fathers are more likely to be protective of their daughters "with shotgun ready" to protect them. Still, society has made some men feel uncomfortable with affection for their daughters. "Admitting I touch my daughters makes me feel like I'm confessing to a crime I didn't commit," said *Dads and Daughters* author Joe Kelly (2002). "Most fathers feel that the joy and comfort they get from hugging and kissing their daughter must remain hidden and unacknowledged lest others be suspicious or mortified," added Kelly. Yet, the fact remains, men can be every bit as nurturing as women when it comes to affection and this affection from the father has proven to be even more important when it comes to raising happy, well-adjusted daughters with good self-esteem. Girls are also less likely to flaunt themselves when the father is involved (Wassil-Grimm, 1994).

## 8

# BETTER SEXUAL CHOICES

This physical affection and involvement from a father may be important for older girls making wider choices in terms of sexual activity as well. Fathers are very concerned about these issues and for good reason. A father closely involved with his daughter is important for the prevention of dangerous and deviant behavior like premarital sex, unprotected sex, unwanted pregnancy, and experimentation with drugs and alcohol (Resnick, 1997). If a father lives in the home, there is a significant drop in out-of-wedlock pregnancies (Whitehead, 1995). There is also a lower risk of teenage pregnancy with a loving, affectionate, and communicative father. In fact, an involved father has shown to actually influence over three-fourths of daughters and their decision of when to begin to have sex (Clemens, 1997). Teen girls who live with both parents are three times less likely to lose their virginity before their sixteenth birthday (Smith, 1994). In fact, older girls who live with only their mothers have significantly less ability to control impulses, delay gratification, and have a weaker sense of conscience of right and wrong (Whitehead, 1995).

## ❧ 9 ❦

# ACADEMIC AND JOB SUCCESS MEANS EARNING POWER

While some studies show a significant bond between a mother and her son, a stronger bond seems to exist between fathers and their daughters, especially as it pertains to success throughout life. In fact, we can ask if daughters can give credit to their fathers for better jobs and higher incomes. That answer would be yes if the causative factor is academic success. One study showed that girls who had positive interactions with their fathers—in terms of love, affection, warmth, and guidance—were more successful in academics and received better grades (Coley, 1998). In fact, according to the U.S. Department of Health and Human Services, girls whose fathers interacted with them were twice as likely to stay in school and not drop out (1993). Girls with an involved father feel more protected, are more likely to attend college, and less likely to drop out of college (Coley, 1998). Fathers who exhibit affection and lay ground rules end up with girls who do better academically as well. Also, girls who have involved fathers have higher quantitative and verbal skills, and higher intellectual functioning than those with fathers not involved (Goldstein, 1982). Therefore, higher cognitive functioning would result in better life choices and higher academic skills would result in higher earning power, independence, and security.

Often, higher education goes hand in hand with financial gains made in life. Additionally, when a father is involved in day-to-day activities, girls are more likely to confide in him and seek emotional support, which leads to effective deterrents against adolescent misbehavior and other deviant behavior mentioned earlier (Koestner, Franz, & Weinberger, 1990).

## 10

# LIVE LONGER AND PREVENT DEVIANT BEHAVIOR

Separation and divorce are hard on all children, especially daughters. Those who experience this tragic life event before the age of 21 will lose four years off their lifespan on average (Schwartz, 1995). Two studies were undertaken with data collected from the North Carolina Population database. The first was to determine a correlation between intact families and children who smoke, drink, or try illegal drugs. The second study was conducted to test intact families and their impact in terms of delinquency and running away, disorder, theft, violence, and use of weapons (National Fatherhood Initiative, 2004). In both studies, "father closeness" was added as a predictor of success and failure. Girls with involved fathers were a "significant and robust predictor" in preventing drug use and their associated activities and whether or not children engaged in these activities and their overall prevention. This is contrasted by the predictors for mothers, whose indicator for drinking sadly moved in the wrong direction. This study then found that not only did intact families have children with less drug and substance abuse issues, but their children had fewer friends with these problems. The evidence was so overwhelming that the researchers advocated improving the relationships and bonds between fathers and children, including non-custodial and non-residential fathers as well. In the second study, the father again was the robust predictor in terms of success and dealing with issues of running away, violence, theft, disorder, and use of weapons. There was also less violence and acting out shown by children whose fathers were involved.

## 11

# SIGNIFICANT STATISTICS

An absentee father also affects the economic, crime, health, abuse, and education in other ways according to the National Fatherhood Initiative. Father-absent homes are five times more likely to be poor, with 38.4 percent of female-householder families living in poverty to just 7.8 percent for married couples (U.S. Census Bureau, 2002). A child with a non-resident father is 44 percent more likely to be poorer (Sorenson, Elaine, & Zibman, 2001). Babies without a father's name on the birth certificate are 2.3 times more likely to die in the first year (Gaudino, Jenkins, & Rochat, 1999). Expectant fathers also play an important role in advocating breast feeding, which has been shown to be important for the immune system and higher I.Q. levels. There is a direct correlation with fathers' knowledge of breast feeding and the likelihood that it was going to happen (Susin, 1999). Single mothers were twice as likely to be depressed as married mothers, have higher levels of stress, and fewer support systems in place, which can lead to difficulty in taking care of a child (Cairney & Boyle, 2003). Children from stepfamilies and single-parent families were more likely to suffer a bump, have a bad fall, or be scarred from an accident as compared to those living with both biological parents (O'Connor, Davies, Dunn, & Golding,

2000). Not living with both biological parents also quadruples the risk of having an affective disorder. Children who live apart from their fathers are more likely to have asthma, an increase for asthma-related emergencies, and a six-fold increase for overall emergency room visits (Harknett, 2005). Father-absent households had a significantly higher rate of incarceration, with a high percentage coming from mother-only households. Plus, nearly 58 percent of women in prison lived without their fathers and had significantly more drug use (Snell & Morton, 1991). Sexually, girls have four times the risk of early sexual intercourse and two and one-half times the risk of higher pregnancy (Quinlan, 2003).

## ❧ 12 ❦

# FATHER'S PREVENT ABUSE

An absentee father is a significant factor in child abuse and doubles the risk that girls suffer physical, emotional, or educational neglect. Girls in this situation are much more likely to be victims of physical and sexual abuse, with a 77 percent greater chance of being physically abused, an 87 percent greater risk of being harmed by physical neglect, a 165 percent greater risk of physical neglect, a 74 percent greater risk of emotional neglect, and an 80 percent greater risk of serious injury from abuse (Sedlak & Broadhurst, 1996). In fact, they had a 68 percent higher chance of smoking, drinking, and doing drugs.

## 13

# BETTER BODY IMAGE

In regards to weight issues and body image, obese children are more likely to live in father-absent homes than non-obese children (National Longitudinal Survey of Youth, 1997). Also, a daughter's body mass index (BMI) was predicted by her father's diet and father's enjoyment of physical activity: as the fathers' BMI rose, so did the daughters' (Davison & Birch, 2001). It is the father's and not the mother's total and percentage body fat that was the best predictor in a daughter's total and body percentage fat (Figueroa-Colon, Arani, Goron, & Weinsier, 2000). In fact, children who lived with single mothers were significantly more likely to become obese (Strauss, 1999).

## ❦ 14 ❧

# BETTER GRADES, LESS DROP OUTS

Finally, as communicated before, fatherless children are twice as likely to drop out of school, but a father's involvement results in their children getting A's over 50 percent of the time (National Center for Education Statistics, 1999).

# 15

# TWO PARENTS ARE BETTER THAN ONE

An absent father almost always means not only less time that the father spends with his children because of being absent, but less time the mother does as well. In a two parent family, dads spend 1.77 hours a day in activities with their children and 2.35 with their mother. With a single parent home, fathers spend 0.42 hours per day with their children and moms only 1.26 hours. Divorce does not increase the time spent with one parent (Lippman, 2004). A study of three- to five-year-olds showed that they were read aloud to significantly less that those families with two parents intact. This slows their reading comprehension and learning ability (Forum on Child and Family Statistics, 2002). Single parent families are also less likely to be involved in school and the education of their children.

## ⇥ 16 ⇤

# RESEARCH SUMMARY

I would like to say that it was enjoyable writing this book for you as well as myself, having three daughters and four children overall. I also have to say that the data is overwhelming in connecting the importance of a father and the very success of his daughter in all phases of her life in a positive and meaningful way. While being perceptively aware that this was the case previously, the statistics and data that came forth were real eye-openers in terms of how important fathers are to not only their daughters, but to their children overall. If we are to make and give lasting value to the human development of our daughters, then fathers must become more aware of how important they are and what their absence could mean to their daughters. We must also make sure that fathers' rights are protected in terms of ensuring a relationship with all their children in the face of resistance. There are those who deem fathers unimportant, and yet this leads to irreparable harm to our greatest treasure and resource, our children.

## 17

# WHERE DO I GO FROM HERE?

That is a good question, and though the facts may seem daunting, there is good news. First, by just looking at the research, regardless of whether you are a daughter or a father, makes the mere awareness of the importance of your relationship become self-evident. It shows that a father is vitally important to the success of his daughter and he should make every effort to make sure his daughter's dreams and successes come true. By the same token, if you are a daughter, you now realize the importance of your father and the need to reconnect in some way with him. Even if your father is deceased or not the ideal father, you can reinvent him in your mind and reach the success that may have eluded you so far. The following pages are what I call the "Solution." In the Solution, there are what I call my "Sweet 16 Tips," which is a guide through 16 secrets for daughters and fathers regarding how to build their relationship and her success. These tips are directed in a way that is invaluable for reaching the goals in life they want to pursue together, essentially leading to a prosperous daughter. In putting this book together, I looked at hundreds of traits I felt were most critical and put them into 16 categories that are the most important for developing an ideal relationship between a dad and daughter, and ultimately a daughter's success. This information should clarify areas you each need to work on to obtain the ideal relationship between a father and his daughter, which is the true intended goal. With this strong foundation in place, a daughter will consciously and unconsciously become more successful.

# SECTION TWO
# The Solution

## Connecting a Daughter's Success to Her Father

CHAPTER ONE

# THE AFFECTION SECRET

"Love is the irresistible desire to be irresistibly desired."
–Robert Frost

Appropriate touch is vital to bonding as a father and daughter. Research has shown that a father showing affection not only affects their relationship with a dramatic positive outcome, but also affects a daughter's future relationships. Simply put, the lack of love and proper affection as a young child and even as an adolescent can influence a daughter to make unwise partner choices as she grows up, as every human being craves affection and attention. However, proper touch, like hugging, helps to anchor love and acceptance into her subconscious. Affection is critical to her acceptance of herself and feeling worthy of love; something that many people search and cry out for their entire lives. Without this acceptance, wrong and unhealthy choices—including drugs, sex, and dysfunctional behaviors—often occur. The fact of the manner is, it is human nature to desire contact and physical touch from others and daughters who do not get affection from their fathers tend to get it in the wrong places from the wrong people. Therefore, it is vital for a father to show affection from an early age on; to give her big hugs, to pick her up and kiss her, and squeeze her before she gets too big to pick up. Simply put, a father must send the message, "I love you. I accept you. I adore you," with his touch.

Common sense stuff, right? Yet the consequences are enormous. Ironically, this proper relationship with affection can also delay or eliminate unhealthy, promiscuous behavior or premarital sex in a daughter craving any kind of physical contact, even if, in the back of her mind, she knows it may have dire consequences. The mother of a daughter should always encourage the father to show affection with his daughter and bond with her. Sadly, some adult daughters report that their father never hugged them, kissed them, and hardly interacted with them. It is no wonder their relationships are so troubled as adults or daughters themselves have trouble in their own relationships apart from their dad's. Even sadder, they often choose partners similar to their fathers. So if they weren't accepted as children, how do they learn and trust any form of affection as adults from others? This is the recycling of sadness, in my opinion. Therefore, while the "strong and silent" father has strengths, he may be leaving his daughter in a vulnerable and unprotected position of trying to fend for herself to find love, touch, and acceptance and that's never a good idea. At this point, she can feel unworthy and her self-esteem will suffer. God gave us the wonderful ability to sense touch, affection, and love and often we don't use it. We must always remember that affection is the ability to show love, not just telling someone you love them. Often, people judge others on their actions, not their words. This is especially the case with proper affection.

Also, there is a special bond that occurs between the biological father and his daughter from early on and it can never be replaced. Not everyone can be put in as a male role model to a daughter. It is difficult, if not impossible, for a stepfather, mom's current boyfriend, or an uncle to take over that role. It may seem adequate on the outside, but on the inside, there is always trouble lurking. Some women are misguided into thinking they can plug a new breadwinner or father figure into place and that she and the new male in her life can provide the nurturing. Unfortunately, this same daughter will always wonder what she is missing and often be resentful if not allowed to see her biological father. My advice for mothers is to allow as much contact with a child as possible provided that the biological father is capable of it. This is not the time to treat the daughter as a pawn and create more problems. Sadly, many adults think of perceived or real spousal hurts rather than what's best for their child, and of course, the child suffers. Also, this is not a slam on stepfather's or anyone else; many are doing the best they can. There is just a special connection there that is similar to a mother and her son. It is a bond not easily broken. Divorced moms are going to have to remember the mantra: love your children more than you hate your ex. So the key to this first secret is for a father to show more affection to his daughter and likewise, for a daughter and the daughters' mothers to demand more affection from the father, regardless of age. It is never too late to create a safe place for a daughter, even if she is an adult. Take the time to reconnect.

Now, for those women whose fathers are dead and/or were abusive to their children and contact is not advised, we need something different. Notice I said "abusive to their children." Usually spouses of both sexes can be abusive toward each other and still be loving toward their children. Also, many parents claim abuse to either themselves or to the child to get back at a spouse or get the upper hand in a custody battle. They use their child as a pawn and essentially harm them this way as well. A parent can also do something that is hurtful to a child, many times unintentionally, but that is not abuse. Being late to pick up a child is disrespectful, but that is not abuse. Stop the pettiness and keep your child in mind. If you're a parent who has to have a child side with you or be on your side in petty battles, you already are a loser in more ways than one.

A new plan must be put into place. In these cases, an adult daughter can take a piece of paper and draw a line down the middle. On one side of the paper in red ink, write down everything you can't stand about your dad and the hurt that has accumulated over the years, whether that ranges from being physically or sexually abusive, to not showing up for a special occasion or a birthday party. On the other side in black or blue ink, write down all his redeeming qualities—his kindness, the times he showed compassion toward you—and his qualities that you admire, like dependability, that he was a good provider, his strength under pressure, his good singing voice, and anything else. Now, cut the paper in half, take a match or lighter, burn the half in red ink, and say goodbye to those past hurts. As it burns, talk to your dad. "Dad, I love you. But what you did was wrong. I forgive you, but I am not taking these negative traits with me and passing them on to my family or my children." Be advised that this exercise could be quite emotional and the tears may come by the bucketful. However, as Forrest Gump once said in so many words, sometimes you have to put the past behind you before you can move forward and look toward your new future. However, leave the negative past behind. If you don't live in gratitude and forgiveness, you will flunk the game of life.

Now take the other half of the paper with the blue or black writing, put it in an envelope, and keep in a special place. These are the redeeming values that you want to take with you, values you can pass to your children, and a new way to look at your dad to increase your own self-esteem. It is not easy to forgive someone when they have hurt you so badly. My friend, Stacy knows this all too well as she relayed to me in a conversation that I will never forget. One day, I was out with Stacy (not her real name) and the conversation turned to her own father. Now, for some reason, I have this innate ability where people want to tell me their life stories. The story she was about to tell me was horrific and one I would never forget. Her parents were Christian singers who traveled across the country to entertain people when she was younger. However, her father led a double life. Through both tears and rage, she told me the story and this is how it went.

"I hate my father," she said. "I essentially became his wife in every way." I sat shocked and stunned. She continued, "Early on in my life, he set up a bed in the basement and we would end up having sex on a regular basis with my mom upstairs. My mother had to know what was going on, but she said and did nothing. Later on, they separated and I stayed with my mom for a while until we couldn't get along anymore. I went to live with my dad, thinking things would be different now that I was older. But they weren't. I did the cooking and cleaning and we starting having sex on a regular basis all over again. I was a confused teenager and I thought I was loving him and protecting him. However, I knew deep inside it was wrong." She continued on, "One day, I broke down and told my mom, since there was no love lost between them at this point. She called the police and he ended up in prison. To make matters worse, his side of the family never believed me and blamed me."

As I sat listening to her, I grew angry, wondering how a father could do so much damage to his own daughter. Also, it turns out that her mom's boyfriends weren't any better. They were always trying to seduce her and sometimes even succeeded. Unfortunately, her mom put her new boyfriends first and either didn't believe her or didn't want to believe her.

As you can guess, due to this damage inflicted upon her, Stacy is in a danger zone for many girls and young women; primed for risky and promiscuous relationships and primed for bad relationships in general with a possible inability to form a healthy bond with a future partner.

Dysfunction has the ability to run deep if it is not corrected. This was not her only fear as well; she said something else that stuck in my head. That people in and out of her family said to her, "I'm just like him in a lot of ways." This is a major concern and how the pattern of abuse develops. People mimic and pattern their behavior with what is emotionally printed on their brains the most and by what they have experienced. Do you know why I want you to do the exercise with the piece of paper? You have to leave the "bad" behind and take the "good" with you. Stacy was clearly at a crossroads. After all, how would anyone be able to drag the emotional baggage and psychic scars through the rest of their lives? It wouldn't be easy at all, nor would it be easy to repair those deep wounds.

I acknowledged her hurts and the damaging insults she had received in her life and listened quietly. I repeated back what she told me to show that I grasped what she was telling me. I then asked her something that shocked her, "What, if any, good qualities does he have?"

Her eyes got wide and she leaned over the table and said to me with anger, "He has no good qualities about him." It was a strong, guttural reaction that was well understood and expected, considering the severe circumstances.

"Well," I said calmly, "you'll need to find something because the connection between father and daughter is so strong that it can affect your entire life. You may not make the same mistakes, especially this severe, but you face the risk of becoming more dysfunctional and making other mistakes and perhaps even may have trouble forming solid relationships, especially with men."

She then had this incredulous look on her face as I think I shocked the heck out of her at this point. She didn't want to find even a few good qualities about her father and who could blame her? "I don't need men in my life!" she retorted.

"See?" I said with a laugh to ease the tension. "It is already happening."

She leaned back and had this look on her face as she scanned her brain trying to determine if I was nuts or onto something. I think she realized I was onto something, although she was not too eager to agree yet. "So what should I do?" she inquired.

"Well," I said, "Tell me some good things about him, there has to be something?"

"Well," she stated, "he is well-liked by everyone, he has charisma, can really sing, and he can take control of a situation and get things done."

"There is your answer." I said. "Take with you the general likeability, the charisma, and any musical talent you have with you along with whatever other positive thing you can find."

I then explained about red ink and blue ink and moving forward. I told her she didn't have to forget what happened, but she had to move forward and find redeeming qualities about her father to live the life she wanted. I am happy to report she is in a stable relationship, has gotten married, just graduated as a registered nurse, and is ready to embrace life. It is hard to forget the insults in our lives, but we have to forgive and learn from them, otherwise we can victimize ourselves over and over again and it will negatively affect and damage our quality of life. So stop being a victim! Everyone can teach you something and somewhere inside, I really believe everyone has a little good in them. You just have to find it; not for their well-being, but for yours.

**The Affection Secret Summary: Daughters need more affection from dads to prevent future dysfunction, but it must be in an appropriate form. Also, find the goodness in your dad and leave his bad traits behind because you will take some traits with you from him, whether you realize it or not. Make sure you take only the good things because you don't want to victimize yourself over and over.**

CHAPTER TWO

# THE GOOD ROLE MODEL SECRET

"We are what we repeatedly do.
Excellence, then, is not an act, but a habit."
–Aristotle

The research is clear on this: if a dad makes bad choices in his life, a daughter is likely to make similar choices. Unfortunately, imitation is not always flattery, especially in these types of cases. This begins in infancy and later as a toddler when a child will likely imitate their parents' words and actions. This is especially true for a father and his daughter. With whatever he says or does, there is a high probability she will follow that lead and eventually become like her dad, both good and bad. Obviously this not necessarily and always true in regards to career choices, but by the way she lives her day-to-day life in several aspects and in other personal areas by watching and observing the way he lives his life.

Unfortunately, as we know with most kids, telling her not to do something often rings hollow. A dad's actions will always shout out more loudly about who he says he is than anything he can say to her. In other words, talking can be effective, but it has its limitations. If a dad abuses drugs and alcohol, the percentage is high that she will too even if he says not to. However, if dad becomes a proper role model and follows his verbal advice with action, chances are much greater she will eventually follow his lead. Oh sure, there may be some rebellion along the way, especially during the teenage years when she doesn't make the best choices. But for the most part, she will follow his lead, especially if she views her father as wanting the best for her. When any person senses the other person wants the best for them, it builds trust. That is the key; does she view her dad as somebody who wants the best for her? That answer is almost always yes, but she must feel it and grasp it before she takes positive action and that comes from a dad backing his words up with action.

Here's another thing to consider: a daughter is also likely to marry someone like her dad. Therefore, it is important for a father to make an honest appraisal of who he is and change the things about himself he views as negative. He can even ask for input here, as awareness is a big part of life for everyone. Another wise thing a father can do is to point out his successes and failures to his daughter, especially how he learned from each experience and how he changed in terms of character. He can show her how these successes and failures help him develop traits like integrity, honesty, and a more loving, protective, and caring nature. Talking about weaknesses builds credibility and strength with the listener. Pretending to be perfect does not do this.

While actions speak louder than words, words can help finish the picture that may be missing. I know one adult daughter named "Kerry" who had relived her childhood experience with me of not seeing her father very much for a three year stretch. She told me that for many years, she always blamed him. Her mom was using her as a pawn and had said if he stepped on her property, she was going to call the police and have him arrested. So he then went through several legal channels to see his daughter. After all the filings, paperwork, extensive time, and what later proved to be false allegations that we see so often these days, he finally got to see her. However, it took a long time to happen.

Once Kerry found out what happened later on in life, her relationship with her mother as an adult soured. "My mom was caught up in her anger and forgot I still needed my father. A good mom wouldn't have put me in the middle. Kids need two parents. I often cried myself to sleep because she made it seem like my dad didn't want to see me. As an adult, he showed me a stack of paperwork and the red tape he had to go through in trying to see me. He even paid child support on time, though it wouldn't have mattered. I needed my dad. It changed the way I viewed my father and my mother from that time on once I found out the truth."

How sad is that? Yet this is typical of the society we live in today. One positive trait that Kerry picked up from this bad experience, however, was that she became a more persistent person—like her father—in going after what she wanted in life. She also learned another lesson: love your children more than you hate your ex. That is part of being a good role model.

Research has shown that the best character traits for a daughter to adopt from a father include emotional strength, courage, intelligence, fearlessness, empathy, assertiveness, and self-confidence. This is why having a father, especially a biological father, in her life is so important. It can affect her very day-to-day existence and success. Think about those traits for a second; you can go a long way in life if you possess them and they are developed through the father-daughter bond.

Of course, all fathers have different levels of these traits and most of them are seen and absorbed through action. Therefore again, those traits that he already has or easily expresses, good or bad, will be much more likely to show up in his daughter. If a dad is weaker in another area, like empathy, a daughter can develop the awareness to reinvent dad in her mind in this particular area or learn to acquire this trait on her own through the awareness of recognizing the traits she wants to have and setting in motion the process of learning how to acquire it. However, it is much easier to do that if dad already has that trait and has expressed it over the years of her life.

So let's talk about awareness. One of the biggest goals in living your life is living with awareness. If you have a clear picture of what is going on in your life and inside of you, you can make adjustments in your own life. Everyone, including both dads and daughters, needs to take inventory of their positive and negative traits and adjust accordingly. A father must do his best to bring out the best in his character traits and a daughter can help him as well in this pursuit and vice versa. Which brings me to some sage advice: it's not easy for people to change, only that person can change if they really want to, and no one can really change anyone else; they must do it for themselves if it is to be long-lasting. However, a daughter can nudge her father in the right direction of having positive traits, thus influencing what she observes in him. This helps to reinforce the development of her own traits. I have seen this happen.

Let's take "Jenny" for example. She told me a story about how her mom was often criticizing her and the way she dressed even though her friends and close friends considered her fashion tastes to be quite modest and conservative. At times as a teenager, it became abusive. "She called me a whore all the time," said Jenny through tears. "What kind of mom does that?" To make things worse, her dad was extremely passive and did nothing at all to defend her. As an adult, the verbal abuse never stopped. One day, she told her dad she was bringing home a young man whom she described to her dad as "fairly conservative and respectful" to meet her parents. Fearing the worst, she told her dad she didn't think it was a good idea and that her mom would still find something wrong with her and this young man. Her father said that he would talk to her mom, but Jenny was not so sure that it would make a difference. "Dad, I appreciate that. But you never stand up to her. That's why she keeps doing it."

So dinner that night at home was uncomfortable for everyone. Her mom barely acknowledged the new boyfriend when he came in and at dinner, criticized her in just about every area of her life. She also punched her in the arm at one point causing severe pain. Her dad did little to stop it, but did mumble, "That's enough." What was mom's reaction? She laughed at Jenny and chided her for being a wimp. After dinner, things got worse. This young man was sitting in the living room trying to stay out of the way when Jenny's mom came around and started in on him about how crappy all men were. "My mom stood over this guy she didn't know and was berating him over and over. It was humiliating and embarrassing."

At this point, Jenny said she saw something she thought she would never see. Her dad got up, strolled across the room, got between his wife and this poor guy, looked her right in the face, and firmly and loudly said, "Leave him alone! He hasn't done anything to you!" Years of living with his passive behavior just left his body and he finally showed some assertiveness. Why? It was because of Jenny's courageous action of asking him to do something to help. At this point, Jenny's mom slipped away back in the kitchen, probably shocked that her passive husband would say anything to her.

Now, I have always believed in unity in parenting and don't advocate verbal confrontations, especially in front of company. But in this case, Jenny's mom got what she deserved. It also changed the way Jenny viewed her father from that point on, knowing her father was going to be on the receiving end of some verbal abuse when she and her boyfriend had left the house. Sometimes a little prompting can bring out the best in a dad. Not always, and you can't get frustrated if it doesn't happen. But sometimes a daughter can help her father be a better dad.

Lastly, the best thing a father can do to be a better role model is to be himself. One of the toughest things a daughter struggles with is her ability to relax and be who she is. Instead, she often becomes what others want her to be. This is at the very core of self-esteem and body image issues. Fathers often have a "what you see is what you get" attitude, without the mask, makeup, and pretense that others can impress upon her from television ads, magazines, and other unrealistic sources of mythical expectations. This is good. Therefore, more importantly, and a big key that I cannot emphasize enough, a dad must be himself, even if that means he likes to watch a lot of football or drink an occasional adult beverage. Being phony creates another list of lifelong problems in itself, as you can imagine, and further creates insecurity in a daughter. It sends the message, "I cannot be myself," and that is passed to his daughter. That is not a good start to life. So remember as I taught you from the previous chapter; take the good traits with you and leave the bad traits alone and behind you. Be thankful for the good traits your dad models in himself to give to you and use your awareness to find the ones where he is lacking, even if you have to reinvent him in your mind or develop them yourself. Your happiness depends upon it.

The Good Role Model Secret Summary: Dad is going to be a role model for his daughter whether she likes it or not. She has to take the good traits with her and leave the bad ones alone and behind. This will help her become a person she really likes and one who is comfortable in her own skin by being and becoming herself. Also, a daughter can help her dad to become a better role model by nudging dad to be better in his weaker areas, which helps her as well.

CHAPTER THREE

# THE LEADERSHIP SECRET

"If your actions inspire others to dream more, learn more, do more, and become more, you are a leader."
–John Quincy Adams

Leadership is an important quality. It gives a person the ability to take control of a situation without being controlling to achieve what they want in life. Furthermore, a father developing leadership in a daughter is important because it helps develop and reinforce her honesty, integrity, and character. It also gives her a rock and foundation to stand on to become successful. Ultimately, that is what true leaders are—honest, with solid character and impeccable integrity. Other things may look like leadership, but are simply a false narrative and may be a pseudo-leadership that is followed because of chain of command, seniority, or because a person has to follow orders. Some of these people may be respected because they are leaders, but if so, they will likely have good leadership qualities and traits to back it up and will not just be relying on position.

What is leadership? In essence, leadership is the ability for a person to get support or help from others to achieve a goal or task. However, it takes the traits I already mentioned to be followed like a leader and other traits as well, like vision, charisma, intelligence, values and behavior. Leadership wins respects, gains people trust, and makes others want to work for them. Therefore, when you have true leadership, things get done, often in an inspirational way, which is the driving force of our society.

When you develop leadership characteristics in a daughter, you develop a person who becomes independent over time, and who doesn't just go along with the crowd without at least giving it serious consideration before she does. You can imagine the benefits of developing leadership in a daughter when peer pressure is closing in from every side pressuring her to do things she may regret but seemed like a great idea at the time. She becomes the one leading the group and helps others find the right solutions and the right road to take. If they don't join her, she makes her own path in life because she is a leader.

Attaining leadership from a father is often one of a modeling nature and by example. There is no perfect, one size fits all type of leadership that works for everyone. Rather, different styles and a combination of these styles work differently for various people.

For example, a father with good leadership skills is neither a dictator nor a passive wallflower, or not even necessarily the strong and silent type. He can be strong, yes, but even silence has its limitations (even though it can be golden in so many areas of life, as we all know). However, in some cases, we can say that being calm and remaining silent and focused can be a good form of leadership. It should also be noted that leadership is given not only by action and example, but by voicing an opinion as well. That's why being silent is not always helpful. Leaders have to be heard at times to give their thoughts and their opinions come from the experience of living life.

Leadership is therefore often a way of making an opinion known to attain resources or to exhibit or enhance the skills needed to be successful at life. Leadership is also the ability to stand for something then taking that knowledge and guiding others to help themselves become more productive than they would be otherwise. With a daughter, a father shows leadership by setting boundaries and making decisions that may seem a little strict to her, but will be accepted if she knows her father stands for something and has her best interests at heart. It is key for a father to understand that he needs to lead for his daughter to learn. In this life, you have to stand for something or you'll fall for anything. That's what leadership is all about.

Good leadership is as old as dirt. You simply give direction and that teaches her to both follow and give direction to other people to help her meet her needs and theirs. Leadership is something she will need to learn in the workplace, if she has her own children, or for other situations that come along in this thing called life. Being a leader also means you have to learn to follow. When you can follow, you simply have the experience to relate to others better. You know what to expect later on from those you plan to lead and what they are capable of. When a father leads his daughter, the daughter then becomes a better leader for her children and those she might be in charge of at work or in other settings. On goes the cycle of success.

What else makes up a good leader? We can say good leaders simply get others to follow, but it is obviously not that easy. They must earn that trust. How? Leaders must first paint a vision of where they want to go and be open and fair with those they lead. They must show they are no better than anyone else and exhibit humbleness. Balancing ego and humility is no easy thing. It is easy to lose a follower if he detects the leader is in it for themselves. You see, followers are not dummies; they can detect insincerity a mile away. Therefore, a leader must lead by example and be dedicated to the task he is asking a follower to do. I call it, "Clean the Toilet Together Theory." If a leader is willing to get his hands dirty, someone underneath may walk through walls for him.

Leaders should also give sincere credit to others to enhance motivation and to keep the vision going. Nothing is worse than someone in charge taking all the credit for someone else's accomplishment. It's another surefire way to lose people who need leadership the most, especially in a father-daughter relationship. Next, integrity is vital in leaders because they get others to trust them and people they lead will know they are guided by their values. Passing up personal gain to help others is a sign of integrity—perhaps passing up a big bonus to be able to afford to keep a coworker or helping a runner who has fallen, even though this takes them out of the race as well. Integrity is about caring about the truth and the other guy as much as a leader cares about his own desires.

Leaders must also use creativity to answer the bigger questions and issues, use assertiveness when deadlines are approaching, and accept accountability for their actions so others will do the same. If they pass the buck, so will others. They must communicate, because this is the basis of all leadership and their actions and words must be consistent. They should even have the ability to use humor to enhance relationships and defuse anger in others. So what does this all mean when someone doesn't necessarily want to create or be the next president or CEO of a big company? Ah, glad you asked.

Leadership passes on the traits to a daughter that ultimately develops in her—higher self-esteem and self-worth. That is very important in how she lives and perceives her life and the world. It will be how she determines if her life has been happy and fulfilling or the opposite. These are critical aspects that a dad passes to his daughter through observation, action, verbal skills, and life experience. They will ingrain into her very being.

However, before you learn to lead—as I touched on before—you must know how to follow. Almost every great leader has learned from someone before him. Every dad along the way has to follow someone—their own mom or dad, a boss, a teacher, or someone else. The experience of following teaches a father what it takes to be a good leader and the traits he likes and doesn't like in the people who mentored him along the way. He then takes this ingrained information and passes this knowledge to his daughter.

Next, every daughter needs to learn to follow direction before she can use these lessons and become a leader herself. This is accomplished by a father giving her choices she can follow. If you are a father, this is really not that scary. The key is to make sure your choices favor your desired end result. Remember, at least she is getting a choice. Sure, she may grumble at first. (Daughters grumble and get an attitude? No! It can't be!). But she will respect you for it and respect is everything in raising a daughter. If a daughter respects her father and he has solid intentions in what he expects from her, that's half the battle and her life will be better for it. As a daughter, do you see the advantage when you have your own kids? I hope so. Being a leader means giving choices, direction, and guidance. It's not leadership to always let a daughter decide what she wants to do, especially in terms of important decision-making. These skills can be lacking if she makes the decisions since the prefrontal cortex is not fully developed.

So here's my message to the "cool" parent trying to let the child rule the home: stop it! Seriously, it is never in the best interest of a child for the parent to be on that level. A dad should be kind, loving, generous, and giving. But he always must be a parent before he is a best friend that always gives in. A smart daughter may like some permissiveness, but inside, she will lose respect for this parent by the minute. Why? Because girls need a security blanket and, deep down, need someone in charge regardless of what they tell you. You've heard about the cool parent; they buy beer and have parties at their own homes for their kids so they can "watch them" because they "know they are going to do it anyway and want to keep an eye on them." Wow, what a defeatist attitude! That may be cool to an 18-year-old, but as they get older, they likely will say, "What were my parents thinking?" Again, every child not only wants, but needs boundaries to build an inner security blanket within themselves. So just remember that being the cool parent usually means failure for both fathers and daughters.

I wish I had a nickel for every kid who said their parents were too permissive. This same kid would also say they experimented *beyond* what they probably would have and paid a price beyond what their peers paid who received proper guidance from their parents. That's why boundaries are important; it says to a daughter that a father cares. Think of it this way: some kids think smoking a cigarette would be pushing the boundaries with their parents. For other kids, they think that smoking crack is pushing the envelope. See the difference? Who do you think will have more problems? That's why a father needs to step up and provide leadership to guide his daughter's decisions as she learns to lead herself. Again, a daughter must learn from her father's example so she can create the success she wants in life, which is the whole point to begin with.

Another benefit of a father providing leadership for a daughter is that it not only sets boundaries and priorities, but it takes the pressure off her. Letting her hide behind, "My dad said I couldn't go to the hemp festival," will probably keep her safer a little longer. Yes, eventually she will be facing decisions on her own in a world that is unkind. But if you can delay those decisions until the prefrontal cortex is developed, she has a fighting chance to make better decisions.

Let me say to any father working and practicing his leadership skills: this is not the time to show and break open the school of hard knocks or tough love on a regular basis. Discipline is important (more on that later in the book), but you have to choose your battles. You can prevent some of the damage to her mind and body until she is older, more mature, and able to make better decisions. A father can and should provide opportunities for her—like a college education or a business venture if financially feasible—but she should be willing to work at it and put in the hours to get it accomplished. If she is not in a position to receive funds, advice, or leadership from dad, that can still lead to other options where she can and should develop the leadership skills to do it on her own. It can also go overboard in the other direction. A father should never give to the point where she expects too much. Leadership means providing her a chance to succeed, but having her earn it as well. She should pass this good work ethic on to her children.

Leadership and following leadership can be tough during those teenage years. Why? Because, as I mentioned earlier, the prefrontal cortex is not fully developed in teenagers and sometimes even into their early adult years. As a result, girls tend to give into their impulses and emotions which leads to not thinking things through and subsequently making bad choices. It is also a time of rebellion. Teenagers seem to think that parents know nothing at this age. Don't believe me? Just ask any teenager. That can mean a rough road for any parent unless you are prepared.

Leadership also means just being there when all else fails. While a daughter needs to learn to make her own decisions and live with the consequences, a father who is simply *there* makes any fall in the formative years less severe. Therefore, leadership that leads to better discipline in a daughter's lifestyle prevents or delays deviant behavior and the bad mistakes until she is ready to strike out on her own. A dad that is there in person can at least present experienced choices and options to her.

Guess what: sometimes they listen, even when they are pretending they aren't. They may be reluctant to verbalize acceptance of direction, but they will be listening and taking it in.

Leadership almost always works better if a father is consistent with it and his actions match the way he professes to his daughter how to successfully live a life. In doing so, the father also earns more respect from his daughter. He must set the example so she'll follow his lead and thus help create a leader in the person she wants to be for the future. Again, you have to learn to follow before you can lead. Dads communicate this from a combination of love and authority, by the ability to follow their own moral beliefs, by not being too upset—and yet, not being afraid to show and express some anger or other emotions at the right time—and finally, by the ability to take positive, assertive (not aggressive) action in his life and demonstrating it in his life and their lives together as dad and daughter.

In addition, solid leadership from her father will give a daughter someone to look up to, to protect her, teach her, help her understand the difference between right and wrong, and raise her expectations in life. Plus, if a father doesn't provide this to his daughter, she'll learn the wrong things from someone else and that is almost a given.

So in the end, it helps if a father is both humble (a good leadership trait) and a protector. There is nothing wrong with a dad letting his daughter know in a variety of ways that he is big, tough, and intelligent and will be there for her. Leadership also means security and this will be more effective if dad is making the right choices as I mentioned earlier and not just talking a good game. Research has shown that daughters love and respond to fathers who are tough—not just physically—strict, but not too strict, and somewhat demanding as long as it is balanced with love, kindness, and affection. Too much of one and not enough of the other is not leadership or good parenting. But in the right balance, it is effective parenting and a thing of beauty.

To put it in perspective, leadership is a balancing act and combination of being assertive and firm without being overbearing and aggressive and possibly ruining her spirit. If a dad is already doing what is right, he should keep doing it, keep his convictions, and be a living leadership example of what he wants his daughter to be. A daughter can learn these leadership skills from her dad or reinvent dad to imagine what he would say about a situation so she can make good choices and live and a happy and fulfilled life. Take the best of leadership traits with you and leave the rest behind.

**The Leadership Secret Summary:** When dad exhibits leadership and teaches her to become a leader, he gives his daughter a foundation to stand on, helps her to resist peer pressure, helps her to take a stand in what she believes in, helps her decision-making ability, and promotes her self-worth and self-esteem so she can have a successful life.

CHAPTER FOUR

# THE PASSION SECRET

"Nothing great in the world has ever been accomplished
without passion."
–Christian Friedrich Hebbel

Now we are on to passion! Do you want to have, or actually be, a successful daughter? Well, one of the most important ways to help a daughter connect to the world around her is to show her how to live a passionate life. Passion is described as that strong enthusiasm or excitement for life that is often combined with intense emotion. Hey, that's how I want to live my life, how about you? The good news is that research shows that if a father is passionate about something in life, it creates a drive in his daughter to be passionate about her life as well. This in turn helps to create positive success patterns that can last a lifetime. Simply put, it is hard to be happy in life without passion. Why is that, you ask? Because passion means you are alive, that you are excited about something, something is making you get out of bed to make life better, and for another important reason: the opposite of passion is apathy, which is the inability to care about what happens and an indifference to change things and make things happen. Wow, does that sound like a miserable life or what? Also, when you are indifferent about life, you accomplish little, you don't smile as often, and life becomes drudgery. An empty feeling forms inside that longs to be filled and it often becomes a life with no purpose, like wandering around in a desert or drifting in a boat without a rudder—always feeling like a victim and at the whim of whatever life throws at you and wherever it may take you. That may be okay if you are in a real boat for a few hours, but in life, not so much.

These passions can be anything under the sun, especially since it really doesn't matter what the passion is. It's the actual action of passion demonstrated in a dad that matters the most because the daughter will likely mimic action of passion as opposed to the actual thing in life that is dad's passion. Although in some cases, they can take on and have the same passion. For instance, a dad may be passionate about mechanics and the dedication involved in working on cars. This work can lead a daughter to be passionate as a nurse, working and tuning up a patient's body. The good thing is that people can also be passionate about almost anything. The greatest athletes, musicians, artists, actors, and business people in the world are driven by a passion to excel and make a difference.

Passion can also make work fun if you like what you are doing. People who have passion open locked doors in front of them. They chase their dreams and are focused on achieving all of their goals in life. Additionally, people who have what I call *positive* passion learn from their experiences, make adjustments, and keep going down the path they have chosen. When a person has this passion in their life, it can help them overcome the setbacks that may come and give them the ability to override the discouragement of friends and family from making their dreams come true.

I just love the word passion. Passion is fire in the belly. It is the ability to propel us forward with that fervor and enthusiasm that says we won't be denied. It is a zest and zeal for something, whether that is a job, hobby, project, person, or thing pertaining to your life. It is the will to win and to drive yourself to be better than you thought you could be. When used correctly, this passion should be for the betterment of those around you. This brings us to one early disclaimer: sometimes passion can be used incorrectly by some people for things that aren't good for them. So what we need is a controlled *positive* passion. I only mean controlled in the sense that we decide the things we are passionate about and yet can help both ourselves and others to lead better lives. For example, a person could have passion about owning his microbrewing beer company and that could be a positive passion. He could also have passion to drink 12 beers a night, which would be a negative passion and unproductive. Yes, I can hear some of you: that may be a productive goal to the uninformed to drown sorrows. But the passion to get drunk is not a successful or productive passionate lifestyle. It is one of giving up and letting the wind blow you off course, not the passion that drives your life to bigger and better heights.

As I mentioned earlier, a dad and daughter can be passionate about different things as long as passion is taught and followed. However, it is sometimes interesting to see a passion that is shared. For instance, in my hometown of Flint, Michigan, there was a story about a father who coached high school basketball. Later on, his daughter and ended up doing the same thing in following a similar career path. In fact, they eventually coached against each other. She had observed from an early age his passion and drive to coach basketball and this sparked an interest in her to first play and then coach. In fact, she excelled as a high school player and went on to play in college. After that, she became an assistant coach for her dad at the high school where he was the head coach before finally before taking over her own team as a head coach later on. It just goes to show you that you never know what seed you are planting in a girl's head that will take hold and help enrich her life.

Also, to reiterate an earlier point, the actual passion a father demonstrates to his daughter can be in almost anything, like a particular job, profession, hobby, or interest in a particular sport. These can be things like astronomy, collecting coins, bird watching, fishing, old movies, baseball, football, or something else. It doesn't matter what it is, just anything that a father gets excited about in life. The important thing here is for a dad to lead by example and be excited about something that gives life meaning. A daughter may not copy the actual activity, but she will take the passion with her and that alone will change her life.

On the other hand, if a father has no passion about life, you may be wondering what happens to his daughter. You guessed it; not much good can come out of this situation unless the goal is to be a couch potato and channel surfing is your idea of success. Passion does not always deal with physical exertion; you can be completely immobile and be passionate about something. However, without a dad being excited about something in life, it's hard for his daughter to be excited about life as well. You get in a state of existing and going through the motions instead of really living.

A person must also remember the difference between obsessive behavior and passion. With obsession, we sometimes don't even know what we are doing or why we are doing it. We lose focus on conscious goals and give way to unconscious and sometimes damaging behavior. We can obsess over food, drugs, sex, or behaviors or addictions that can damage the body and soul. We crave some things that are not good for us. Now, passions can be positive or negative, but obsession takes it a step further toward destruction. I know one teenage girl—let's call her "Jo"—that was obsessed with everything having to do with her face. She was gorgeous to begin with, but if she got a blemish on her face, it was the end of the world. She scrubbed, bought cleansing masks, and used several products on her face. She did okay controlling the skin issues and like many women, developed an intuitive sense about which of these thousands of beauty products actually work.

However, a situation developed that she couldn't control: her nose began to grow. It was supposed to, right? She was growing up. But that's not the way she viewed it. Through the eyes of a teenager, she saw it as disfiguring to her look. After this, she became a nervous wreck, avoided mirrors, tried to shape her nose with her hands to almost mold it into form, and covered it with her hand at various times. To me, I could hardly notice the difference. She looked beautiful. For her, however, this led to an emotional breakdown and a string of medications and psychiatric help to get her through this situation over a period of several years. Finally, when she grew up, not only did she come to accept her nose, she actually liked it. I'll talk about body image in another chapter, but you get the picture. If you are passionate about being beautiful and healthy, fine. Just be careful that obsession doesn't take you over the edge.

Another important aspect to consider is that if a dad is actually present as we discussed before and does things with his daughter, this helps to activate the passionate "gene" in her and helps her hang on to a secure figure as she begins to explore life. I am a big believer that kids, especially daughters, need their dads around so much so that if a divorce happens, everyone involved should make sure a good co-parenting agreement is place without the emotional baggage that two parents bring to this situation. Let me say again: love your children more than you hate your spouse. This means have the biological dad around to connect with the children because this is vital to the success of children, again, especially his daughter. When he is around, she can observe his passion and simply put, if a father has passion for life, his daughter will also. It is contagious. It's really important that no matter who you are, you need to pursue something they really want to do and pursue it with passion to help connect to the world. Another point to be made is in terms of work or occupation: if you do something you love, the money usually follows and it doesn't become work at all. Maybe not always, but with no passion or enthusiasm to do something, you don't have much fun and life is not enjoyable. Make it enjoyable, find your passion, and if you are a daughter, start by learning from your dad.

Here's another problem facing single parent households where dad is not present. A daughter wants and needs to know how her father sees life, how he explores it, what experience is telling him, and what pitfalls she can avoid. It is virtually impossible to fill this void without him as her mother can only do so much. No matter the reason for a breakup, a daughter needs to know the male perspective of life that comes from her biological father. Brothers, uncles, stepdads, and the latest boyfriend will never fill it completely. This is just like a son will always wonder about his biological mom who is not around or may have died even though a step mom may be raising him and doing an adequate job. It is that innate biological and genetic connection of who made us and where we came from that will reign supreme. That's not to say these other male figures aren't doing the best they can, it just is not the same.

A daughter learns about life by seeing dad's passion that makes life worth living. If a dad has passion, he gives his daughter a bigger purpose for life. Sometimes even a romanticized vision of her future is better than not giving her any vision at all. I used to ask my oldest daughter, Caroline, when she was a young child of four what she wanted to be when she got older. She would always confidently reply, "I want to be a star."

"Oh," I would say, pretending not to know what star kind of star she was referring to, "like a star in the sky?"

"No, daddy." she said, "Like a real star—a movie star."

Believe me, she meant it. Now, realizing that very few get to that type of level and having my own hopes as a professional athlete dashed early on, I could have doused her dream with reality, but I was smart enough not to. I picked her up, gave her a big kiss, looked her in the eyes, and as seriously as I could, said, "Peaches (my nickname for her), you can be anything you want to be." And guess what; I meant it. As an adult, she has model and movie star good looks and she could still be a star and always will be in my eyes. To impart this positivity and believe in a child is a wise choice for any parent because it helps to imprint on her subconscious that she can do anything she wants to do in life. Who are we to say she can't reach any dream? After all, the only way to reach a dream is to go after it.

Some people instinctively have unstoppable passion. But for others, the question should be asked: how does a person create passion? This can be accomplished by developing an interest in life through their own eyes and by being around the people, things, books, and music that enrich their lives and create the desire to want more, while avoiding the negative people that douse the flames of passion and excitement in life. Passion is also best enhanced when it is shared with others. So get excited about life and live with enthusiasm by looking forward to it and by spending time around people who are passionate themselves. One key is to have something in mind you look forward to that stirs the fire in the belly and gets you motivated. You will know when you are there. Others will notice it and you will command attention from others because you will be more animated, your eyes will get bright, and you will know inside that you can't be deterred. When you can feel it on the inside and others can see it in you, even what you say can and will become important and people will listen. That is the power of passion. When you believe in what you are saying, you will able to sell your greatest commodity—you. If you can get excited about you and what you want, others will get excited as well.

Once passion is attained, it leads to bigger desires and a clear, bigger purpose in life. If you discover what your passion is, then you can use it to discover what your life and perhaps what your life's work will be and look like. Again, for the most part, passion is about doing what you love and as I said before, if you do what you love, then the money will follow in terms of a career. This comes from developing that unbridled passion about something that moves you. But passion is not all about a job or money or a hobby. It is about living life to the fullest way possible—the way God intended you to live your life.

As I said earlier in terms of passion, it helps for a father to give his daughter both a realistic and a romanticized passionate vision of her future because this is what dreams are made of. When dreams can become reality, this is, again, better than not giving her any vision at all. A father should also know it's okay to share what he sees in a daughter's future and give her guidance based on his own personal experience and then let her incorporate her own passions into her thinking process. Believe me; a daughter will develop her own set of dreams on her own. If the dreams that a dad has don't match his daughter's, he need not worry because he gave her the ability to dream and chase her passions in the first place. By doing so, a father enables a daughter to take on the world. After all, life should be lived with passion, not fear. Also remember that one of the most important things a dad can do is to show her his view of the world and help her connect to it so she can develop her own passions and interests. As philosopher Alfred Souza once said, "Dance as though no one is watching you, sing as though no one can hear you, love as though you've never been hurt before, and live as though heaven is on earth." To me, this is passion. If you find positive passion and enthusiasm, you have found one of the best reasons for living.

**The Passion Secret Summary:** A daughter needs a passionate example to follow from dad to help create success patterns and help make her dreams come true since she will always follow his lead, consciously or subconsciously, or even follow her own unconscious ideas. However, make sure her passions don't become obsessions. Give her a vision and let her have her dreams. After all, it is about living life to the fullest.

CHAPTER FIVE

# THE ACTIVITIES SECRET

"The future depends on what we do in the present."
–Mahatma Gandhi

As research has shown us, one of the best kept secrets in developing a successful daughter is for her father to spend quality time with her and for both dad and daughter to get involved in various projects and shared activities together. This exposes the daughter to how the biological father thinks and acts and how he makes decisions. This is not about having a perfect father making perfect decisions, but rather a biological father as a human being making some good and not so good decisions. Regardless, a daughter will always wonder how her biological father thinks and that cannot come from strangers or a third party. It must be observed, if at all possible, from dad himself. Every human being has something to offer.

Now, spending time together may seem like an obvious thing to do, but you would be surprised at how many fathers and even daughters overlook the importance of spending time together. Sometimes there is interference from someone else preventing a dad and daughter from being together. This is why I encourage moms to get involved early to promote the bond and activities between a daughter and her dad. This, in turn, produces more successful and positive outcomes for their daughter. A mom, especially a divorced mom, should always love her child more than she hates her ex-spouse. Simply put, a dad spending quality time with his daughter as a child helps her to build a bond with those she loves, promotes and builds her social skills, and makes the world a little less scary, especially if he takes her out into his world so she can interact with people and perhaps even different people than mom brings into the picture even if they are together.

Also, a father may know he loves his daughter in spirit, but doing things together is a reassurance of love and builds trust. It also shows her that he will be there not only mentally, but physically when things don't go right for her. Love is more than words, it is action. When a dad becomes present, he becomes someone you can depend on. Love is a fickle thing. When you love someone, you not only tell them, you have to spend time with them to show them and strengthen that bond if it is possible. It isn't always easy, as I am sure there are some long-distance dads that unfortunately cannot spend the kind of time with their daughters that they would like to. This is where co-parenting together and creative scheduling is of paramount importance regardless of the relationship of the parents.

The great thing here with the activities secret is that it is never too late to do things together, although it certainly is a huge benefit to start when a daughter is young. What can a father do? How about going for a walk together, heading to the movies or to a restaurant, playing kick ball, basketball, soccer, or any other things that may interest your daughter? My daughters love to go shopping. You can never go wrong there, unless you are trying to buy tires for your car and bore her to death. However, even if you have to buy tires for a car, you can still spend that time with her and maybe buy ice cream on the way home. The point is, just do something that is interesting where you can spend time together. The point here is that you are together.

Still stumped on what to activities a dad and daughter can do together? How about some other fun activities including building and flying kites, camping, board games, photography, teaching her to ride a bike, surprising her with notes and letters, building a treehouse, teaching her how to play a musical instrument, looking at nature through binoculars, or checking out the moon with a telescope? Dads like to boat and fish as well, so take her. Activities can also be adjusted as a daughter moves into adulthood and throughout her lifetime.

However, probably the best "activity" a dad can do with a daughter is to listen. As Larry King liked to say in so many words, "I never learned anything while talking." All dads, especially those who are not real talkers themselves, need to spend time looking into their daughter's eyes and listening to them in a receptive manner, or listening when they write something, text something, chat something, or e-mail something. Especially important is in person on a one-to-one basis where listening really comes into play. By the same token, a daughter who *really* listens to her father builds their bond even deeper and learns a lot. So spend time with each other and honor each other's presence. After all, just being together is an activity that helps builds confidence and self-esteem in a daughter and will help to make her successful. Just remember, listening is indeed a powerful skill that all people need to master. I'll have more on this in the communication chapter.

Attending an activity or function can make a huge difference in a daughter's life. By contrast, not attending can leave lasting scars. Take Jocelyn for example:

> My mom and dad divorced when I was young and my mom gave my dad a hard time. Every time they talked, she was yelling at him about something and living in the past. To make matters worse, she wanted me to embrace her new boyfriend as "daddy" and I wasn't having it. He wasn't my dad. I'm sure my dad got frustrated because of the constant arguments when he picked me up or dropped me off. He said he didn't want to rock the boat, although I didn't know what that meant at the time. I still saw him, but less than before and sometimes he didn't show up. Then the time came for the father-daughter dance. My mom wanted me to go with my stepfather and I decided I probably wasn't going to go. A couple weeks before the dance, I saw my dad. I held his face with my two small hands and with tears running down my face, I begged him to take me to the dance. He said he couldn't promise, but would do the best he could. It didn't sound

convincing but I looked him in the eye and said, "I know you'll be there. You can't worry about mom; I'm your daughter." I asked him to pick me up at 6:30 p.m. on Friday. The day of the dance, I got dressed up like a princess and was waiting for my dad to show up. Well, at 6:32 p.m., I was anxiously looking out the window and he still wasn't here. Mom was already getting on his case in the background, saying he wasn't going to show up and yelling at my stepfather to get ready. I sat looking out the picture window with a few tears rolling down each cheek, but still hopeful. A few minutes later, I looked up and my dad was pulling in the driveway! My heart was pounding in my chest. "He's here! He's here!" I exclaimed and ran to the door to meet him.

Jocelyn continued,

He was only a few minutes late, but my mom was jumping on him the minute he hit the door, asking him where he had been. He looked her straight in the eye and said, "I came right from work, but I also had to stop and pick something up." Then he pulled out a red rose for me and a fresh corsage he had been hiding behind his back. I jumped up in the air and was now beaming, and so was he. We went to the dance and had a great time. He was so nice and treated me like a princess. We went out for dinner and ice cream and it was awesome. It was also the weekend so there was no need to get me home early as he had tried to do before to keep my mom happy. As he dropped me off, he started to get another earful. This was when he finally stood up to her. "She's my daughter too and things are going to change!" He wasn't aggressive, but assertive. And things did change. Instead of worrying what she thought, he put me first and he showed up more often. My feelings for my dad changed right then and there and it continued to get better over time. I learned from him that sometimes you can't worry about the grief you'll take. You have to put your daughter first and also stand up for yourself.

Stories like Jocelyn's are why I tell dads to hang in there and fight through the grief of opposition. Try to do what's right. If you buy her a doll house, don't sit on the sidelines in your La-Z-Boy chair with a cup of coffee and a newspaper. Get down on the floor and get on her level. It's all about being a dad she will never forget if you make the effort. So be playful and have fun and get active in her life. After all, you won't get this time back. Adult daughters should be aware of this as well. Just because a dad says he's okay later in life, if that keeps you from seeing him as often as you should, find the time and make the effort to do so anyway. Dads can be silent when the face of pain and disappointment comes their way from those who are supposed to love him. Doing things together also helps to set the tone for a daughter as she gets older, interacts with others—especially the opposite sex—and develops important social skills related to these very activities. Again, a dad should start doing activities with his daughter as early as possible to build a bond, promote security and social skills, and build a lifetime of memories.

**The Activities Secret Summary: Dad should be involved with a daughter's activities from an early age to reinforce and reassure love and to build trust. It should be remembered that although words are important, actions speaks louder than words and sometimes listening is one the best activities they can do together. Most importantly, a dad must fight to stay involved in her life despite obstacles and the best way to accomplish that is by doing activities together and by a dad putting his daughter first.**

CHAPTER SIX

# THE COMMUNICATION SECRET

"Don't find fault, find a remedy."
–Henry Ford

Communication is critical to the success of any person and that is especially true between a daughter and her dad. It also comes in a variety of forms, with the most effective being non-verbal rather than verbal, although both are critically important. However, the real key is grasping and understanding why communication is vital to begin with, especially between a father and a daughter, while also further grasping the importance of starting communication early in her life so trust is developed over time. Research has shown when a high level of trust is developed between a dad and his daughter; it leads to better choices and healthier outcomes in all areas of a daughter's life and for the duration of her life. Much of this trust comes from something very important—communication.

Effective communication is important for many reasons. It is vital to enhance relationships between almost anybody, including family, friends, spouses, and co-workers. But is especially important for a parent and a child and even more so for a daughter and her dad, as I said earlier. Research has shown that daughters do care what their dads think and also look to the experience a dad provides. Though they may not readily agree with what their dad may say, they are almost always listening and taking it in. It also means that a daughter takes much of what she sees and hears to her heart, so much so that all men that come into her life later on will be judged, at least subconsciously, by how her father has communicated with her. As you can imagine, for her, this sets up further expectations for and from other men she will come into contact with in the future as she walks through life. As you might also expect, this can lead to either good or bad outcomes based on this early communication with dad.

Great communication is also important because it allows a person the opportunity to listen well so they can reflect and send back a message that is well-received. In fact, listening and not speaking may be the most effective form of communication. It allows the person on the other end of that message the ability to feel that they are heard and understood. When this happens, it further boosts self-confidence based on acceptance. Why? Because we are often accepted simply based on the way we listen, communicate, and try to understand others.

Though people may disagree during a conversation or through other forms of connecting, with effective communication in place, their opinion still matters and is being listened to. Because of this, we as people can share our opinions with less of a chance of judgment and misunderstandings developing. It also means we can disagree without being disagreeable. This is an important tool to learn and can be carried down from dad to daughter.

As one grows in learning effective communication, this person's self-esteem will also tend to increase over time, sometimes dramatically so. In fact, effective communication is vital to everyday living, enhances a person's worth to an employer or a company, and also increases both personal and job performance. When there is a lack of proper communication between individuals, there is a drop or gap in information that develops that can negatively impact a person's life in all areas. The importance of communication should be obvious to all.

Think about it: we are all "salesmen" in a sense. We have to sell ourselves continually in life, whether on a resume or even to our spouses or our own children. In fact, the methods and ways of communicating seem to be endless. As I mentioned earlier, it can be in person verbally or non-verbally, by e-mail, phone, Facebook, written or typed letters, sign language, touch, fax machine, instant messages, Twitter, MySpace, or ranging from high-tech to the most simplistic of forms. However, learning to master the basics of solid communication helps no matter what type of communication or format is actually used.

Good communication should include and allow for feedback and be a two-way street where people take turns sending and receiving messages. It should also be positive and effective whenever possible to prevent further problems. Why? Do you know what one of the biggest complaints that negatively affects the work environment? You guessed it: poor communication. This kind of communication blames, incites, points fingers, increases frustration, and decreases job performance. In essence, a home is like a work environment as well and negative communication does not help a family thrive. Therefore, it is inexcusable not to learn these skills because good, effective communication is the road map and vision for both an organization and any personal relationship. Don't think so? Think again, because with a few choice words, you can lose a job or a friend in a matter of seconds. Contrast that with the synergy, unity, and togetherness that good communication provides those that want to meet new occupational goals or further enhance personal relationships.

In addition, the female way of communicating needs should be considered when a dad is dealing with a daughter. I personally have learned a lot about communication with women through trial and error and success and failure. Sometimes, just enough clues are left that you can figure some things out. For instance, most women don't want someone to fix their problems, they want them to listen. Why? They have pretty much already decided what they are going to do. They are usually just looking for confirmation or reassurance. Of course, with a younger daughter, you need to get in there and fix some things based on the underdevelopment of that darn prefrontal cortex. However, that doesn't work with adult women so well. (I hear every woman reading this chuckling right now.) Next, women need acceptance in communication. You can compliment a woman a thousand times, but to them, it is like they are hearing it for the first time. By contrast, a criticism can be said once and remembered forever. This is because people, especially women, tend to remember the negative things about them because it "appears" to them to be true even though it may not be. So criticism, even constructive criticism, can appear harsh to a woman even if you have her best interests at heart. For example, if a woman asks if she looks "alright" in a dress, a smart guy would say, "You look gorgeous and terrific. That dress was made for you." If she says, "Do you think my butt looks too big in these jeans?" he better come back with the right answer there as well or pay a heavy price! A daughter can be the same way and they think they already know what you are going to ask before you actually do. Of course, some males have the same gift; that's how I know they think like that! So a dad needs to listen to a daughter and gather facts before he tries to fix a situation.

As I previously mentioned, listening is a major key and the beginning to all good communication. A breakdown quickly occurs when you conclude or assume you are right and others are wrong, you do not allow the other person to finish their sentence because you assume you already know what they are going to say, or you misinterpret what others are saying because you are not actively listening carefully. So many problems in the world between different people, races, and genders could be solved if people would just be quiet, listen, and reflect back for clarification. Sometimes, the other guy or gal just wants to make a point and be heard, so just let them say it. This helps the listener as well, who must first absorb all the ideas and the perspective of others during a communication effort before making up their mind and coming to a conclusion. Therefore, it is better to pause and think before making accusations or saying something you will regret. If you are a person that has trouble communicating about yourself directly to someone, you can use stories and examples of others to take the heat off yourself, then focus on listening and gathering more information. If someone perceives you are talking about yourself, admit it. Honesty wins the day in communication.

The following are some key points to remember with the communication that occurs between all people, especially between a dad and a daughter. Since dad has the life experience, many are geared to helping him in how he communicates with his daughter. But a daughter should take these with her as she moves on during life to pass down to her kids:

- When you provide and express feelings and thoughts, share your rationale. For instance, "because I said so" has limited effectiveness when kids are younger and less when they become teenagers.
- Encourage feedback and active involvement. Actually ask them how you can help the situation. This will allow them to open up and share their thoughts on the situation. You should also ask them if they have solutions in mind.
- Listen to the other person with empathy and respond the same way. This shows you care and are receptive to what they are saying. Clarify what the other person is saying by repeating back and by asking questions to show understanding of what they are actually saying to you.
- When discussing issues, provide as much support as you can without removing responsibility.
- Maintain and even enhance self-esteem if possible when communicating.
- Make it a conversation and do not "grill" or conduct an interview. This puts people on the defensive. Direct confrontation shuts down communication. Better to say, "How was the basketball game?" as opposed to, "Did you meet up with that boy I don't like at the game?"
- Watch their body language. This is always a dead giveaway to what they may be thinking or if they are telling the truth.
- Try to be as non-judgmental as possible and try not to overreact. This shuts down communication.
- Remember you are their parent, not their friend. Their safety comes first instead of trying to be the cool parent. However, you should have her friends over and know who they are, as this can reveal much about who she runs around with and sometimes the kid who doesn't belong to you may even fill in details.

Sometimes the situations can be more *critical* and require extra steps. Whenever someone like a daughter faces something or someone they feel is hard to overcome, it helps to do the following:

- Keep and maintain their perspective in place: "Losing 'X' (whatever that is) is not the story of your life." (For teenage girls, breakups with a boyfriend can be traumatic).
- Humor is always good to defuse anger in some situations, but it has to be well-timed and only used in situations where it is well-received.
- In a tactful way, explain that life goes on and that they should dig down and look for solutions. That may seem simplistic, but it is the truth. Life does go on and they need to fix their issues.
- Help your daughter to respond to situations with dignity. For example, you can teach her to look at a breakup differently by telling herself, "We both saw the relationship differently. But if he wasn't happy, even though I was, I have to accept that and move on."
- Encourage her to live her life one day a time and that these problems will pass, especially with a good plan.
- Tell her not to be afraid to say to say she was sorry if she hurt someone else. This shows strength, not weakness.
- Teach her to stay away from complaining and condemning other people over their actions, especially if those actions are in the past. People are human with human weaknesses. Criticizing them won't change the circumstances.
- Ask her, especially if she is withdrawing, "What are you thinking? What are you feeling?" Withdrawal can be a sign of depression or even suicidal thoughts.
- Encourage her to not be a victim. When something bad happened to me, I would meet up with someone and joke, "You know how I am doing. How are you doing?" That usually relieves the tension.
- Always encourage prayers. God is there to help her. Make sure she knows that.

Another important key to good communication is to have as much live, face-to-face time as possible. All these forms of communication I previously mentioned don't replace live contact and person-to-person interaction. I can't emphasize that enough, so schedule your time together if you have to. A dad should always be available to talk and listen without judgment. Later on, an adult daughter should make the effort as well. This will give a dad a chance to take everything in and offer advice or solutions down the road, even though many times they just want someone to listen to and not fix their problems, especially when they become adults.

We previously talked about how a dad needs to be a good model for his daughter. The same is true in the communication department. A father needs to be that example his daughter can follow when communicating. This means being an "open book" as much as possible, which means being honest with no secrets, being a trustworthy source to rely upon, and by being someone a daughter can easily communicate with and approach when she wants to talk about something.

Communication also goes back to what I said before about a father simply being who he is more than anything else. This means if a dad has the ability to handle stress properly, can guard against negative actions in speech and behavior, and has the ability to resist porn, drugs, and excessive alcohol and other negative vices, he *communicates* to his daughter which kind of actions and behaviors should be emulated and which ones should be avoided without saying a word. This is important because actions and values are emulated at a deeper level than speech and lectures about how one should live their life.

As I mentioned earlier, communication should start early, but it is never too late to start. Dad should give a hug to his daughter often (which is physical communication) and pick times to talk with her during the day. There are many more moments than one may realize when he can find time to do so, especially at bedtime as he reads her a story, as he talks to her in the car to take her somewhere, during a commercial break while watching television, when they stay up and watch a movie together at a commercial break, or maybe during the movie if it isn't a very good movie. Just anything and anytime to stay connected to her.

Praying with her builds a special bond and is another form of communication. Praying is important because the bible says whenever two or more are gathered, God is among them. This gives hope because it encourages one another, it helps to heal those that are sick, and it help to strengthen the bond of walking through this life together.

A dad should always tell her she is special. Why? If a dad can communicate that she is special, she will want to do the right things to please her dad; not always, but enough of the time. As she gets older, a dad can write letters and continue to be a good listener because these are the things that will win a daughter's trust, love, and affection. Therefore, if a dad is smart, he can help guide her to the right decisions while making her feel she owns that decision. A dad can do this by staying engaged, consistent, loving, kind, and as always, by asking questions.

Some communication questions to ask teenage daughters: Who are your friends? Are your friends sexually active? Do you have a boyfriend? Do your friends have boyfriends? Are you sexually active? This will give a dad some basic information to work with. Above all, especially in times of despair, a dad should put his arms around her, ask her if she is alright, and just spend time with her, even if that time is silence during a difficult situation. If a dad builds a good connection with his daughter, she will tell him the things he needs to know to keep her safe and build closeness between them.

Just being silent and letting someone speak can also be an effective form of communication. As you can surmise by now, I like to give advice, but a valuable lesson from my good friend "Mary" taught me the importance of listening to other's advice. Maybe I was a little tired that day, so instead of being talkative and jumping in with my thoughts, I decided to listen attentively. A few days after this meeting, I ran into a friend of hers and she related something startling about the talk I had with Mary. "Mary said it was one of the best conversations she had ever had," this friend said.

That caught me off guard and I smiled and said, "Oh…ah…yes it was." I didn't even know what else to say and I was assured it was not a joke. I thought back and scanned my brain and could not think of anything spectacular or noteworthy I had I actually *said*.

Then I ran into Mary and started to joke with her about the "best conversation she ever had." However, she quickly conveyed to me she wasn't joking. "You didn't say much at all, but you reflected back my thoughts to me, clarified what I had said, and listened like you cared about what I was saying." Interesting, she felt I was a good conversationalist because I just reflected her thoughts back to her in terms of clarification. This helped her feel that I was really listening. Wow, were my eyes opened. The truth is, you don't have to talk a lot to be considered a great communicator. You do, however, have to listen.

**The Communication Secret Summary: Effective communication leads to positive outcomes for daughters, enhances all relationships, improves self-esteem, and is vitally important for success in life. Sometimes the best forms of communication are not the spoken word, but rather non-verbal cues, listening, and even well-placed silence.**

CHAPTER SEVEN

# THE CRISIS SECRET

*"When written in Chinese, the word 'crisis' is composed of two characters. One represents danger and the other represents opportunity"*
–John F. Kennedy

B efore we proceed further, let's define some things. Passion is the desire you put forth toward living your life. Resolve is the determination inside to make things happen on a daily basis; to reach your goals. Sometimes when things get kicked up a notch and we meet more resistance, we get to crisis, which are those big bumps in the road that successful people must learn to maneuver around. In fact, major factors in how a daughter turns out in life is how her own dad handles crisis in his life, how she perceives he handled it, and how he teaches and helps her to handle crisis in her own life, either through his own action by setting an example or by his guidance.

What is a crisis? A crisis is a turning point or change in someone's life that may affect them forever and can be seen either positively or negatively based on their perception. Some of negative examples include divorce, breakups, suicide, paralysis, serious illness or injury, perceived disfigurements, financial stress or struggles, loss of sexuality, and loss of friendship. Some events can even be seen as a positive crisis, like sudden fame, sudden fortune, or things that may be overwhelming to them but seemingly desirous to others. Also, some things like divorce, illness, or injury can be seen as positive if it changed their life for the better. I know one guy who had a stroke from a high-pressure job and spent most of his recovery time watching kid's baseball games at a nearby field from his wheelchair. He eventually recovered enough to start walking, switched professions, and started coaching youth sports, including baseball. He actually said that the stroke was one of the best things to ever happen to him. Without it, he might still be stuck at a tedious, high-pressure job.

These crises can be considered serious or not serious, but this is often determined by the person going through them and is often influenced by their personal life experience. For example, getting acne for some teenagers could be classified as a real crisis to the young person going through it, but perhaps insignificant for an adult with similar issues but more life experience. A person who must give a speech for an award may be envied by some, but this may cause extreme fear in the actual person going through it with a real fear of public speaking, making it a crisis for this person. As I mentioned previously, a perceived crisis should be defined by the person going through it. Also, not only is perception an issue, but much is based on the person's resolve and self-esteem in terms of getting through a crisis. Therefore, a dad who has built resolve, passion, and self-esteem into his daughter and a daughter who strives to learn these traits will create a person up to the challenge of a crisis.

However, getting through a crisis is not a simple process. Many crisis situations are often unexpected events and that makes them all the more difficult to handle. Also, some people are good under pressure while others collapse, further changing the dynamic of handling a crisis. Experience is also a valuable teacher when going through difficult times. Hopefully a dad has learned from his previous experiences in life the proper way to guide his daughter in this area. If not, he needs to grow in his ability to handle adversity so he can be an example for a daughter who will be watching and observing him closely. I know for myself that over time, I have grown to not only survive, but to thrive in pressure situations and ultimately those are the things that contribute to a daughter's ability to be successful in life. There were times I made mistakes, was misunderstood, and treated in a way where I felt I was looked upon as unforgiven, either because they didn't have all the facts, they didn't care what the facts were, or they thought they knew all the facts. But they didn't, and I was confident of that. There were other times when lies were told about me with the intention of purposely hurting me so that it would affect my personal and professional reputation. I learned that life was cruel and because of half-truths, I have lost people I thought were my friends. Now, you may think that is a sad story, but guess what: I found out who were my real friends were, both in and outside of my family. The fact is that I wasted many nights with tears and sadness until it turned to anger and resolve.

As a reminder of my newfound resolve to get through the crises in my life, I bought a great white shark tooth and put it on a chain. It was my personal way of saying I am no longer the hunted because of mischaracterizations, but now the hunter. And that's what I became. I quickly stopped wasting time on trying to prove anything to anybody and spent little time with these people or worrying about the anchors trying to hold me down. Essentially, I became free. I quickly eliminated the dead weight and sought out open, friendly, and nonjudgmental people who chose to listen and be opened-minded about my life. Of course, not all these people knew they were eliminated in mind from my life. Why? I had decided to have a smile for everyone and chose not to waste another day explaining their flaws in their thinking or even my flaws to them. I just didn't spend much time around them, or if I had to, I smiled and went on my way. That's when life got a whole lot better.

Let's be clear: life is not easy and there are no guarantees. So it is vitally important, as I previously mentioned, that a daughter learn from a father's actions and his guidance in how to handle all the adversity, despair, and tough times that occur in every person's life. This is especially true since few people can get through an entire life without crisis happening and also since she will be modeling his behavior either consciously or unconsciously. That is why action is so critical by a father and goes back to modeling. A dad can *tell* his daughter what she needs to do to handle the conflicts in her life, but she will learn more and likely mimic his *actions* and reactions to the crises that come up in his life. Therefore, it is not enough for dad to simply tell her to keep her chin up. He must show her how he keeps his chin up when things are not a bed of roses for him. I am smiling as I write this because I know what you are thinking: in theory, it sounds so easy. In practice, it is a whole different game. But consider this, it is not only a worthy investment into a daughter, but critical to her success.

Okay, so how do we handle crisis? Rule one in handling any crisis is to draw the people around you closer together. A dad shows leadership when he makes everyone around him understand that even though that they are going through a tough time, they are going through it together. This is an important lesson for a daughter to learn. When things are going wrong, they need to come together and stick together. This doesn't mean that everyone won't need alone moments to sort things out in their head. However, nothing is worse than isolating yourself for long periods of time or separating into cliques or factions and pointing fingers at each other. Sadly, that very thing happens every day. Some people just have a real inability to handle the stress and adversity that both life and crisis brings and they want to break off into factions and attack each other. You see it in marriages and various personal and business relationships every day. It seems easier to blame others but in the end, this person loses because it rarely solves the problem at hand and people have long memories of what you say or do to them. It is a lesson that finally sank in for me. Better to walk away being kind and with a smile than create World War III.

Now, when it is a daughter or even a dad that goes through a crisis, it's important, as I just mentioned, to stay connected and bond together. Just based on age alone, a dad has likely been through enough life experiences, crises, and real adversity where he can help her look at all these situations with a realistic calm, resolve, and reassurance that this storm will pass. This staying together and not pointing fingers at each other or others is the first step toward getting over a crisis. However, she must first understand that it will pass and that the trauma is temporary even though the damage is permanent. It is similar to an injury; some see no hope for the future and take a multitude of adverse actions that can complicate the situation even worse, like taking drugs or alcohol to sedate oneself from the pain or even going as far as committing suicide. Certainly these are not ideal ways to handle the rough spots in life and yet we see it far too often.

So far we have established that any crisis or loss can be devastating and no grief or crisis is necessarily small when it is your own. We also know that loss is often defined in the head and the heart of the person affected. Therefore, we next need to understand that the grief stages—shock or disbelief, denial, anger, bargaining or guilt, despair, and acceptance or hope—can vary in degree of severity in each person and as I mentioned earlier, can be triggered by things and situations that would not give others a second thought. That's why I mentioned a teenager will become obsessed with a pimple or the size of their nose and an adult may not think twice about it. But then again, they actually may. Why?

It is based upon on how every person sees themselves into adulthood based on their self-esteem and self-acceptance. Certainly there are many adult women who are obsessed with their looks and body shape throughout life, but even so, many also have realistic expectations of themselves. It is those that do not that can become troublesome and dysfunctional. However, I will have more on this and body image later. I could give you examples of more serious crises that I briefly touched on like divorce or paralysis, but I wanted to show you that even seemingly minor things can blow up over time if the stress and the situation is not reduced and dealt with. Therefore, we should not discount someone else's situation as minor.

Another important step in handling crisis is the freedom of expression. A daughter should be allowed and encouraged to express her feelings of perceived or real suffering and sadness, and these feelings should not be ignored or minimized by others. This expression is important because it allows both crisis and loss to be handled in a healthy way where feelings about the situation are acknowledged or verbalized and which may or may not lessen the sting of an event. If not expressed properly, these thoughts and feelings can be burned into her subconscious in a negative way, which then affects how she lives her life and the choices she may make in the future. As any older citizen reflecting back can tell you, life is all about the choices we make. In short, it can also negatively impact her self-esteem. Withholding feelings can also lead to further shame and dysfunction. Why? Because if a child or a teenager cannot express their honest feelings and emotions, it may signify a dysfunctional family or poor interrelationships where true expression is expected to be bottled up and a young person is forced to deal with these events on their own. That's why it is important for a dad or any parent to have patience, which is always a virtue in raising any child, especially a daughter. Why is patience important? How many times do we as parents want to shut down when we listen to a child because they appear to making a mountain of a molehill or we have heard a similar story? Therefore it is important to just listen and see what they really are trying to say because listening may uncover something important that needs to be dealt with and if not, it at least strengthens the bond of communication.

Therefore the best way a dad can help in terms of communication during a crisis is twofold. First, a daughter's crisis should be listened to without judgment. Second, he should acknowledge her pain. Listening without judgment will often allow someone to say even more about a subject or event that they may have been afraid to share. This means that in the end, a dad get more facts about what is going on. When a dad recognizes her pain, she will often feel that she is not in this alone, even though he may not grasp the depth of the pain. Next, even though there is a situation where she doesn't want to talk, being there for her through the tough times reinforces her security and acceptance of herself. It tells her, "If my dad says this will be okay, it will be." Also (I covered this is in a previous chapter), listening, for a dad, doesn't necessarily mean always giving advice. I learned a long time ago from the women in my life that sometimes they want me to just really listen so they can vent instead of necessarily trying to fix things either by some action or by giving my opinion or advice. This was another light bulb moment; they pretty much know what they want to do. They just need to express it to confirm their own feelings or actions.

There are other ways of dealing with these negative or stressful situations. For some, diversion is especially helpful when a crisis strikes. For instance, writing a letter to get your feelings out or to even change the subject or conversing with either a close friend or perhaps a person outside of someone's social circle may help to protect privacy issues. Growing up, I had my own ways of dealing with crises. For me, being outdoors and being physical helped. I like playing basketball and doing some gardening. These were and still are cathartic releases that allow me to release the stress during a tough time and help me to think things through. Music is another great option I depend on. There a multitude of options that people can turn to. The point is, release the stress and think things through clearly.

A smart dad is one that can draw his daughter closer to him rather than let her isolate herself, as I have explained. However, there is a balancing act here as well. She needs time by herself to think about what is happening and possible solutions to lessen the sting when going through a crisis. Coming from a different perspective, a dad can light the candle of thought in his daughter, but the slow burning of the candle during the night is comparative to her thinking about the situation. It won't be easy because all daughters eventually try to test a dad's authority and knowledge especially during bad or difficult times or in the teenage years. But a dad needs to hang tough and show courage to be there for her when she is going through this adversity. It does pay off if you do.

A typical crisis for a daughter, like a teenage breakup or the divorce of her parents, can be very harmful and damaging to her, leading to more burdensome problems during a critical time of psychological, emotional, and physical growth. It can be especially damaging if a situation like a divorce leads to her seeing her dad less and therefore having less emotional support available to her to help her get through it. It is important to realize that kids should not be used as pawns by one spouse and kept from the other parent. One spouse disliking another spouse is not a reason to keep a child from seeing the other parent. In fact, doing so can cause anxiety, depression, and may even cause the child to blame themselves for situations they have no control over, like a divorce. Furthermore, as I mentioned previously, it is not an easy task to help a daughter through a crisis depending on her age because a daughter can see the previously-mentioned events as the end of the world.

These crises can be multiplied in intensity and effect if one parent is using their children as a pawn.

So let me say this here: I have never understood the need for one divorced parent to have the child see the other divorced parent as they do through the negative and damaging lenses of divorce and bitterness. This is damaging and toxic behavior by this parent and a form of parental alienation. So let me say it again: love your child more than you hate your spouse. When you do this, you will feel better about yourself and happier that you are truly making a positive effort in co-parenting. This is also when I tell dads to hang in there, even if the other parent is hard to deal with. A dad needs to fight for his kids and sometimes for his marriage. Here's something that may surprise you: kids would rather have their parents together and arguing than divorced and apart. Why? The loss of a parent, especially a biological parent, is devastating to their psyche. The old notion about it's better for the kids to be taken out of a situation if their parents are not getting along is a fallacy. It may be better for the parents, but divorce and separation is devastating for the kids even if they agree it is best for both parents and kids often blame themselves when parents split up. Kids from rocky marriages do better than kids that are from divorced parents. So be careful who you marry, be careful who you have kids with, and try to make it work. Also, abuse factors go up for a child from divorced parents. I will talk about that later in the book along with the devastating consequences of divorce.

Another critical reason for handling crisis situations effectively is because suicides peak during this time of adolescence. Though suicide rates have slowed from their peak rates of the 1980s and 1990s when divorce was becoming more common, it still has doubled since the 1950s and 1960s when nuclear families were more intact. For those in the 15 to 19 age brackets, suicides have more than tripled. Also, since suicides for adult men and women have dropped some in that same time frame, it becomes evident that our children are the ones really suffering today, especially from divorce. It should also be noted that during this critical time period, the frontal lobe is still developing, which can lead to some unwise decisions. There may well be crises before this critical age and after, but the teenage years are some of the most vulnerable ages for girls. Prevention is critical because suicide is almost always a permanent solution to a temporary problem.

Also, statistics show that nearly one-third (30.4 percent) of girls seriously consider suicide and close to 12 percent actually attempt it, with grades nine through 11 more likely to attempt suicide than a twelfth grader. Apparently, impending graduation gives them a flicker of hope for the future. Here is something else to consider: there are more suicides than homicides in the United States, which means that sometimes the biggest battle to overcome is the internal battle. So again, this means that what becomes important is suicide prevention. So what does a dad look for in preventing suicide? Consider this: nearly 70-80 percent of those who die by suicide exhibit some of the warning signs, which include:

- Giving away their favorite possessions.
- Losing interest in life.
- Acting sad or depressed.
- Struggling with school or work.
- Intense shame or guilt over events, like being abused, a divorce, or a breakup.
- Drawing pictures or writing about suicide or death or writing a will.
- Change in eating and sleeping patterns.
- Abusing alcohol or other drugs.
- Social withdrawal from friends, family, and activities.
- Behavior, personality, or mood changes. Acting out, acting impulsively, or being reckless.
- Feeling helpless, hopeless, or expressing rage or anger.
- Stating things like, "People would be better off without me."

Don't be misled by someone who smiles or appears to be happy. Once they have made up their minds to attempt suicide, they may be euphoric or giddy, and give out a false impression that they are happy. They may smile a lot without real resolution to their problems. The reason this happens is because at this point, they have accepted what they feel they must do. Therefore, we must do everything we can to help them and always remind them that suicide is a permanent solution to a temporary problem for a problem that can be fixed over time.

So the real answer is learning to handle a crisis before it gets too far and people feel hopeless. This can be done through a series of questions that a daughter can ask herself or, depending on her age, you can do together:

- Can I change how I look and feel about this crisis?
- What factors can I change about this crisis? What things must I accept?
- How can I manage my stress until this crisis is over?
- Who can I express my feelings to where I can feel safe?
- What is my gut feeling about this situation and how can I change it for the better? Women/daughters are very intuitive.
- How can I evaluate the ongoing crisis so I can see that I am making progress in resolving it?
- Am I implementing changes that are necessary to resolve the crisis?
- Do I know when I need someone to intervene if I get stuck? Can I ask for help when I am overwhelmed? Who can I ask for help?

If your daughter or anyone else is experiencing a crisis, get out some paper, jot down the questions, and answer them as best you can. Putting it in writing and continuing to refer to it (adding to it if need be) helps to monitor and track progress. This also brings awareness to the situation and focuses on what action steps need to be taken. Remember, handling a crisis properly might be one of the most important things a dad can do to help his daughter get through it.

The Crisis Secret Summary: A daughter with no dad may feel she can accomplish things in life, but life for her will never feel secure or safe. Feeling safe usually means the ability to get through a crisis. The key here is not letting a crisis turn into a major obstacle regardless of how serious it is. If this can be achieved, a daughter will boost her self-esteem and resolve and be more successful in life. Since a daughter mimics her father's action, he must be a good role model when a crisis arrives and handle it well. How? This can be achieved by sticking together, not pointing fingers, avoiding isolation, expressing feelings, and by monitoring both progress and danger signs.

CHAPTER EIGHT

# THE DISCIPLINE SECRET

*"The first and best victory is to conquer self."*
—Plato

There are two disciplines I want to talk about the most in terms of daughters and dads. First, there is the discipline and correction a dad gives his daughter so she can grow as a person. The second is the self-discipline she will take with her throughout life that helps her to succeed.

Without these disciplines, real achievement is much harder if not almost impossible to attain. This can lead to the inability to reach those goals a person really wants to strive for and achieve.

Why is this so? This is because discipline is often tied to learning and boundaries in the first example, while the second example is tied to sacrifice and hard work, which is at the core of much success.

So let's start with the first discipline I mentioned, which is about teaching your daughter, not punishment. It is the ability to train your child to make good choices from an early age thus giving her the ability to learn appropriate behaviors so she can successfully function in the world. This first type of discipline also involves setting boundaries in a clear way, as this gives a dad the ability to maintain his authority and his daughter direction without him being overbearing. As this happens, a daughter becomes accustomed to the rules and laws that surround her and this guides her life and helps keeps her safe as she gets older. This discipline should also start at an early age. For instance, as a child approaches a hot stove, should a parent let them continue forward until they burn themselves? Of course not. There are some things they will learn on their own, but other things must be taught. For example, they must be taught right from wrong, to be kind to be others, and how to respect other people and their possessions. Have you ever had a prized possession you loaned someone come back in worse shape than when you gave it? That's because that person probably needed to be taught to respect other people's things and came up short.

Additionally, all people need the discipline to respect others and who they are. The truth is, a child must be taught this type of discipline. It is not attained by simply crawling around on the floor and by hopeful osmosis. You've heard the phrase, "Spare the rod, spoil the child." It simply means that without discipline, the child becomes a taker instead of a giver and expects the world to cater to them. This leads to unrealistic expectations and failure because they will turn into a person no one wants to be around.

Harsh discipline is out. I am always amazed when people continually beat their child to attain conformity and simply wind up just breaking their spirit. Instead, discipline is using common sense and tools like timeouts on young children as they are able to understand they did wrong and taking away privileges as they get older. Although I really don't think an occasional spanking hurts and may actually help to get their attention in some cases. However, the end goal should always be more about correcting behavior with empathy and love. A child should feel like you are disciplining them because you love them and are concerned about the situation. If the child grasps this, discipline becomes much easier.

Another important reason for proper discipline is that the prefrontal cortex portion of the brain is not completely formed during adolescence. So it stands to reason that a teenager will make more decision-related mistakes and many of these mistakes would be impulsive or errors that an average older adult would not make and which could lead to some serious consequences. Therefore, it is actually cruel not to help a daughter toward positive outcomes with the guidance and the decision-making tools obtained from a parent, especially her dad. However, it should also be noted that this discipline and guidance is not always welcomed. (What 18-year-old doesn't know more than her parents?) Therefore, a dad should pick his battles wisely and learn to teach his daughter self-control over self-indulgence and selfishness. This ultimately leads to better decisions by his daughter.

For example, if a daughter exhibits inappropriate behavior or clothes, or is swearing or mean-spirited as she grows into the turbulent teen years, imagine both the emotional intelligence she will acquire and the advantage she will have throughout life if this is dealt with promptly through proper discipline. She actually learns what is appropriate and inappropriate over time. When she masters these boundaries, she becomes more personable and reliable to others and has more successful relationships. Then later on, because of her ability to build successful relationships, she likely becomes a person with a successful career or job as this discipline outcomes positively affect other areas of her life as well.

With time, a well-disciplined child becomes self-confident in their world, knowing what can help them and what can hurt them. They learn to control impulses to stay safe and to function in a healthy way guided by the inner compass of experience and discipline. In fact, God has encouraged parents to discipline their children, which then creates a safety net and security a child wouldn't have otherwise. Without it, a litany of psychological illnesses can develop in terms of unhealthy emotions and dysfunctional behavior. Amazingly, many children, even those raised in a permissive household, come to crave discipline even though sometimes they don't realize it. You would be shocked to learn how many therapy sessions begin with, "Well, my mom and dad weren't around much so I could do what I wanted." This is a recipe for failure and even many of the kids know it. When kids don't have experience, they desire someone to be in charge and look for the experience of someone who has walked a similar path at some time, even if it is a parent.

Also, as I have talked about throughout this book relating to a daughter, whose behavior will she model? That's right: dad's. So a father must be consistent in both his behavior and how he disciplines his children. If he can discipline properly and be a role model of self-discipline for her to emulate, they are both ahead of the game. Unfortunately, in real life and without parenting guides on every end table, progress is made by both parents through trial and error, especially since there is no one set way that works for every child. For instance, you can just look at one child and they will start to cry. Another child will show little emotional reaction to being exposed to a stronger discipline. A father, or any parent, in fact, must know their child and how they react to different situations and discipline. Again, discipline is to correct behavior and help with self-reliance. It is not to be punitive and to break the spirit.

There are two keys to keep in mind when disciplining your child for correction. First, be consistent with all discipline. Secondly, follow through on whatever you tell your child. Failure to do these two things is one of the biggest mistakes a parent can make. Following through is the key to changing future behavior so it not a constant tug of war battle between a parent and his/her child. In fact, the discipline you carry out today and how you implement it helps to predict future behavior of a child both tomorrow and farther in the future. If not done correctly, it leads to a crying, resistant child who throws constant temper tantrums, gets in arguments, and pushes a parent's buttons. Is that what you want as a parent? I didn't think you would.

So how does follow-through work, you ask? Pretty easily. You have to pick your battles, it has to be realistic, and you have to follow through and do whatever you say you are going to do as a parent so the child knows you mean it. For example, if you want a child to put a toy away that he or she left on the floor, you say, "If you don't pick that toy up and put it away, I will pick it up and put it away for the rest of the day." Then, if the child doesn't pick the toy up, the parent should do exactly as they promised and put it away and not get it out for the rest of the day regardless of any ensuing tantrum or resistance to the parent by the child. This is the follow-through on doing exactly what you say you are going to do. When the child learns that the parent is serious about they say they are going to do, the behavior of the child will change. When a parent does not follow through as I mentioned earlier, then fights and arguments rule a parent's daily life in terms of discipline. Notice the punishment is short-term and not applied to other toys. It is specific and direct. When age appropriate, you can ask them to pick up all their toys. If they do not pick them up, put the toys away for the rest of the day. Whatever you do, don't mention anything you can't follow through on, because this is where most parents fail and fail miserably. For example, saying that we are not going to get ice cream or we are not going to the movies if you don't do x, y, and z, when you know darn well you are going there regardless of what you say or do, undermines your ability to discipline when you really have to do it and damages your credibility with the child. Also, if you don't follow through with this, you may think it is okay for that day, but they will think all future demands and requests are up for debate as well. That debate can take the form of anything from that annoying cry you can't stand, to the continual daily resistance that will drive you crazy over time. Now, certainly there are some things that may require longer lengths of time of discipline to get the message across. Perhaps cheating on a test would require being grounded for a week or taking away the beloved toy gadgets and video games for a similar time period. Just make sure the crime and consequences fit together and it is not so excessive as to ruin the spirit of the child.

Another important key element of discipline for a dad or any parent to master is the ability to offer his daughter or other child at least two choices when asking them to do something so they are involved in the decision and also an active participant in the process. This tactic can help with getting better cooperation at a faster rate of time because a child may feel they have a voice in choosing what they have to do. Essentially the two choices are both things that dad wants, but since it is presented in a choice format, his daughter will likely choose one so that her dad will tend to avoid the argument and the time-consuming power struggle that a child will try to pull him into. For instance, if a child is slow to put their toys away, you can say to them, "Well, we can both sit here and you can continue to play with your toys or we can go out and get ice cream. But we can't get ice cream until the toys are picked up and put away." Therefore, the parent isn't making the choice per se, the child is making the choice on whether they get ice cream or not. This way, a parent builds cooperation and as I mentioned earlier, it helps to avoid temper tantrums and other bad behavior once the child knows you are serious. This method also sets up consequences for the child and they come to realize that choices in life do matter. However, if you are the parent that gives in quickly because you want the ice cream more than the kid does, you are going to struggle. Hopefully you do not have a rum raisin addiction and you can follow through. Here are some other strategies in approaching discipline for a father, including some I already mentioned:

- Never approach any situation with anger. Allow yourself a chance to calm down and take a level-headed approach to any situation that may come up.
- Use good eye contact and listening skills. Teach your daughter to do the same.
- Follow through with anything you said you were going to do in terms of consequences.
- Explain that all actions have consequences, both good and bad. Good choices and obeying brings benefits and disobeying brings the opposite effect.
- Present what you need from your daughter calmly, firmly, clearly, and assertively, but never aggressively.
- Never threaten or promise a consequence you don't plan to follow through with.
- Focus on the problem or issue, not on your daughter.
- Avoid screaming, yelling, and excessive physical punishment. Don't over-punish or discipline.
- Never condemn or criticize who she is personally. Don't break her spirit.
- Pick your battles wisely or your daughter will stop listening.
- God said, "Spare the rod, spoil the child," and this is true. However, you have to pick your spots and only use this method to get her attention. If you find yourself spanking on a regular basis, you are probably doing something wrong. Focus on your teaching methods.
- Find them doing something right and give them praise and rewards. They will seek that kind of positive reinforcement again if you give it.

- Many children act out in the face of indifference. If you ignore them, they will act out in a negative fashion. Children seek attention and if they can't get it from doing something right, they will try to do something wrong to get your attention.
- Make sure you know she is forgiven for whatever she has done and that she will learn from this experience.
- A well-placed bargaining tool can be useful. For instance, if you say, "If you behave well at Aunt Mary's, we can get ice cream after." Then only do it if they behave.
- Be a role model in your behavior if you expect her to follow your lead. She will model action every time before words.

Another type of discipline to consider that a daughter needs to know and incorporate and should be taught from her father is self-discipline. Nothing worthwhile in life can be achieved without it. While many people talk about self-discipline and working toward their goals, it isn't easy to do and many struggle to develop and get better at this skill and eventually get side-tracked. What is self-discipline? It is the ability to change your future by the choices you make today. This often means putting away things you might rather do right now to do things you *must* do to succeed. In fact, great is the person who can push away immediate gratification to focus on long-term goals to reach the perceived greater and more satisfying achievement of tomorrow or sometime in the future.

I heard someone sum up self-discipline this way: "If you are hunting elephants, quit wasting your day stepping on ants." A person can start out having great goals and dreams to pursue and then find themselves getting caught up in the many mundane and trivial things in life, wasting precious time trying to achieve what they set out to accomplish. Therefore, people must be aware to get rid of the distracters in their life if they plan to reach their dreams. For instance, if you are on a diet, eating pizza or ice cream may delay you in reaching your goal to lose weight. Therefore, self-discipline would mean foregoing this temporary pleasure and focusing on what you really want to achieve. Imagine the self-confidence and self-esteem boost one would have if he/she could conquer this area of his/her life and over the immediate gratification that comes in the form of food, sex, and drugs—things that, not surprisingly, a person will often use to medicate themselves from their own pain. Self-discipline helps you to choose against and overcome these negative behaviors. In some cases, it means letting go of the negative people that are bringing you down and raining on your goals. However, this does not mean a boring lifestyle, but rather the ability to persevere and see the bigger picture that leads to happiness and satisfaction.

If a person can focus their thoughts and behaviors and continue to take consistent action to attain a goal, then they have exhibited self-discipline rather than acting on impulse. It is this ability or inner drive that allows one to achieve greatness and avoid the apathy and laziness that leads to failure in achieving goals. A daughter needs to understand that she has to work toward a goal and that sometimes that means, as I mentioned before, making sacrifices. With training and time, a daughter can master some if not all of the elements required to put in the time to achieve the self-discipline needed to reach the goals she wants to achieve in life. I know I sound like a broken record, but a dad needs to model self-discipline behavior in his own life as well. Let's be clear: it helps if he is a living example of self-discipline because this is behavior she will tend to model.

Another important point to remember is that self-discipline is not meant to cramp someone's lifestyle, but rather enhance it. It is not about *not* having fun, but rather having *balance* in work and play so you can have even more fun in the future and more satisfaction in achieving something. For instance, it is hard to buy a boat or a trip without the self-discipline it takes to make money and pay for those things we desire. Therefore self-discipline is all about perseverance. This means when obstacles come, a person does not quit. Instead, they keep fighting and increasing their resolve toward their goal when distractions come their way. Now imagine the benefits when you do reach a goal. You stand a little taller, you feel a little better, you have more self-esteem and confidence, and you feel more satisfied and happy. You have focused, preserved, and accomplished something. What can we achieve with self-discipline? Just about anything we want. At least professionally, I have always admired Arnold Schwarzenegger. Why? Imagine the self-discipline it took to win seven Mr. Olympia bodybuilding titles through constant training and dieting, to become a movie star in America with a foreign accent, and also become the Governor of California. This does not come close to conveying all his contributions in his professional life. How did he do all of this? Through self-discipline. He trained his mind to achieve his goals and to sacrifice where he needed to. There is a lesson there for all of us to understand. If you want the big things in life, focus on the big things and make the sacrifices and effort to reach those dreams.

**The Discipline Secret Summary: There are two types of disciplines that a daughter must learn from a father. The first is the discipline of correction using follow-through to help her grow and keep her safe in the world. The second is self-discipline, where she uses sacrifice and foregoes immediate gratification to help her reach her goals and dreams. Both disciplines help boost her self-esteem and confidence through accomplishment.**

CHAPTER NINE

# THE DATING SECRET

"I have never let my schooling interfere with my education."
–Mark Twain

A h yes, the world of dating. Now here's a subject not every dad looks forward to talking about or dealing with in terms of his own daughter and probably for good reason. That's because most dads remember being teenage boys on the prowl themselves, how their own hormones were going through the roof, and how they were sizing up every blossoming female that passed by as a potential conquest. I actually thought I had solved this potential dating "problem" for my daughters by deciding and subsequently telling my daughters that they would not be able to date until they reached 43 years of age and, of course, by shining up my shotgun to ensure that very thing would happen. Oh well. It's funny how those intended plans sometimes don't work out. Unfortunately, the best thing a dad can realistically do is to put strategies in place to protect his daughter as much as possible in the dating scene. So let's talk about those strategies.

As you can tell by my subtitle, an education in handling a dating daughter is not just based on the formal schooling one is taught from psych books, what a daughter is telling you she is doing or going to do, or even that you can trust her when she pleads her case. It goes further into your own education of what is real, relating to your own experience, and

I what would laughingly call, covert operations. Again, it goes back to prefrontal cortex not being fully developed and the potential of wrong or poor decisions being made by a daughter. It's not that you want to spy on your daughter (too much), but you should have some guidelines in place to protect her and her future. It also doesn't mean that some boy has to be perfect to date your daughter either because that hardly ever happens. Now, I might add, if you haven't figured this out yet, this is directed toward the teenage daughter about to enter the dating scene, which I believe should not begin before the age of 16. In my opinion, there is simply no good reason for a girl to date before the age of 16 and nothing good can come from dating before that age. Yes, I am aware that some have gotten married when they were 16 or even before and have been married for over 50 years, but these days, those successes for that age are few and far between. In fact, the average teenage girl may think she is in love five times or more before she hopefully escapes the teen years unscathed and discovers what true love is.

The next important thing to keep in mind is a dad should meet anyone his daughter dates and have her understand that you would like to meet anyone she goes out with. Why? Anyone she doesn't want to introduce to her dad could be a potential problem. Certainly some girls will feel you are prying or being nosy by asking who she is going out with, but in this day and age, she must be made to understand it is a necessity. It is a dangerous world that we live in. Dad can help ease that pressure she feels by promising to not give a potential suitor the third degree when he arrives. Dad can also explain to a daughter if a boy is willing to meet her parents, this means he has the potential to treat her with respect and this is something she should want for herself. It doesn't have to be a long drawn-out meeting the first time, but rather simply coming in the front door, saying hi, and introducing each other to start out with. Meeting a boy and her potential date face-to-face is rule one. Of course, for safety reasons, it is always good to know what this boy looks like.

Imagine the opposite of that. Some girls who suffer with self-esteem issues can actually cling to boys or other people who treat them badly. This leads me to my next point: never let a boy honk the horn of his car to pick up a girl, especially if it's your daughter. If a boy is afraid or unwilling to get out of his car, come up to the door, and look a parent in the eye, then he could be trouble and just after your daughter's body. How do I know this? I am speaking from the experience of having been a teenage boy with a car. It is hard to admit this, but there were many times I did that. I simply didn't want to face a girl's family knowing that in a few hours we would be having sex once again and that I really didn't have interest in their daughter beyond that. Sadly, there are also some girls' families that simply don't care and will let a boy spend the night in their own house. They become so engrained into the prevalent "cool," permissive family atmosphere of today that the rules and morals become so relaxed to the point that what obviously should be the difference between right and wrong is simply tossed aside like an old pizza box.

The next important step is to set a curfew. I believe 10 p.m. when going out with friends is okay and around 11 p.m. if on a date, dependent upon the time a movie lets out. (Preferably an indoor movie, if you catch my drift.) Some events may require some time leeway, but this also does not mean a later movie should or can be picked by a daughter and her beau so she can stay out late and beyond curfew time. Of course, there will be times when curfew can be changed if there are special reasons for her to be home early and you can add or restrict time based on their ability to stick to their curfew as a daughter earns trust. In this instance, the element of trust is met by something very simple—meeting curfew times. It is a daughter's responsibility to tell a dad where she is going, when she will be back, and to call him if there is a change of plans.

A couple of things to watch out for as a parent include a daughter calling during the evening and asking to extend her time right before curfew is up or, if with friends, asking to spend the night at someone else's house. (She wouldn't have the courage to say she wanted to spend the night with a boyfriend, would she?). When she asks to stay out later, although not always, it usually means things are about to happen that would make you angry if you knew about them. This is where you have to stick to your guns as a parent. Having a curfew actually helps a daughter to have the ability to say "I have to be home" to avoid things that are uncomfortable. Many kids even like the "out" it gives them, anyway.

In terms of coming home late from curfew, a few minutes of grace period (perhaps 5 minutes, but definitely not more than 15) is not problematic unless it becomes habitual. At this point, she is testing you and trying to push your buttons. Her promptness invests or withdraws from her trustworthy account. You can also further restrict curfew time if she is late multiple times in a week. For example if she is late three or four times in one week, cut the curfew time by a few hours the following week. If the lateness keeps going, then restriction of phone and dating is appropriate for a limited time. Or since she had to be where she said she would be, you tell her you will come get her if she is 15 minutes late. You don't want to break her spirit, embarrass her, or get her to the point she wants to run away. However, you do want her to become accountable for her time and actions. Why? This will help create a very successful woman into adulthood who becomes both accountable and prompt. So it might be nice to buy her a watch to help her out. Ha!

Another part of the dating inventory is to gather facts about her social circle and ask her about the people and friends in her life *before* she goes out on a date. The reason for this is that peer pressure is enormous for today's teenagers and it is good to know what you and your daughter are dealing with. So this is the best time to casually ask her about people in her class and if they are dating, having sex, what they think about dating, etc. This is not the time to give her the third degree or you'll end up with defensive or evasive answers. Also make sure she knows that you have her best interests at heart and aren't trying to ruin her fun or cramp her style. You are simply looking for honesty to help her make some wise decisions to protect her. Also remember this: this is an area where she is looking to see if she can trust you and whether she can divulge more information. If you play hardball, she may clam up. However, depending on her personality and the trust you have built with her, you might be surprised by what she tells you and that information could change the direction of her young life.

Another strategy I like is the "get out of jail free card." If your daughter gets caught up in a situation that is uncomfortable and she feels stuck, she can call you to come get her with no questions asked. If you do pick her up, don't make her feel guilty for asking you to and don't rip her boyfriend or other friends to shreds. For instance, what if she did get stuck in a situation where she was drinking and there was not a safe driver to take her home? Would you want someone who had been drinking to take her home? No, you wouldn't. What if a boyfriend was trying to put the moves on her or she ended up in an environment filled with drugs and she felt uncomfortable? Would you want her to tough it out? Of course not. You would want to do more to help her. If you build love and trust in your daughter from an early age, don't be surprised to see her take you up on that offer. This does not mean she is not responsible for cultivating responsible and trustworthy relationships. It just means that sometimes kids find themselves in a situation they have a hard time getting out of and in the end, it's just about the end result and not the anger. So get her home and be thankful she trusted you enough to call. That doesn't mean that at other times it might not be different; she might need to see some emotion and even anger based on the situation. But at key times, give her that out, do what you promised, and build that trust. If you do, you could save her from a very bad life-changing experience.

So, when should that awkward sex talk between a parent and their child actually happen? Obviously before dating starts is the right time to discuss *desires* with a daughter, especially physical desires. Here is another key: you must follow through with this discussion even if she says she doesn't want to hear it or even that she already knows what is going on. Why? First, a dad's responsibility is to share and follow through with his opinion and beliefs about all topics, including sex, and he needs to let his daughter listen to what he has to say. Secondly, studies have found that even if she acts like she is not listening and seems annoyed, she is still absorbing the info you are sharing into her brain for future reference, even if she doesn't acknowledge it. The key then for dad is to plant and discuss the understanding of not only her desires, both emotional and physical, but that of the hormone-raging boy she will have to face as well. Oh, what fun it is to be a parent. So what are the rules for talking about sex to your daughter?

- Find an easy and comfortable environment to talk to her about sex because it may be a little embarrassing for both sides. In many cases of communication, you do not want distracters. In this case, however, at least to start out, it may not be so bad. Driving in a car where you are looking out the windshield and she is looking out the passenger window, in a mostly-empty restaurant, sitting on a park bench, or at home watching television as you clarify something you don't like that you see there could all be ideal locations. What you are doing is giving her an out—a chance to look out the window of a car, at a menu, at the people swimming in a lake, or stare at the television. Once the communication has grown to a level of more trust, you can sit and talk with her anywhere and perhaps with more eye contact. However, sex is a powerful topic and no matter what she is looking at, she will listen.
- Make all talks free from real interruptions—no cell phones or computers for either one of you to be distracted by. She may look elsewhere, but real distractions are out. This is one case where texting or talking to her friends prevents her from listening and in these cases, she is communicating with others, not you, which is different than what I mentioned above.
- These types of talks rarely start too early in life, but they must be age appropriate. Young kids may have questions about their bodies and where babies come from. Teenage girls may want to know about sex and boys. Teach your teenage daughter that sex is a healthy and pleasurable foundation of a committed and monogamous relationship. (If you are like most dads, you want this to happen later in life—much later. So tell her that this happens when she gets married at the age of 37 and check out her reaction. It could be priceless!)
- Be honest and use correct names for body parts. Don't overload them with information they don't understand. Ask them what information they already know and what they are confused about. Honesty leads to better listening by a daughter. Sometimes humor can be used to communicate in awkward situations as well. What you know about sex as a parent is less important than listening.

- As both a Christian and a person who wants something special for his daughter regardless of those personal values, I believe it is proper to teach them to wait for true love and marriage. There are many regrets over bad first experiences: at least this is what is being reported by many girls. Quite frankly, she deserves to be happy. A dad should explain the benefits of waiting and that regardless of what her friends are doing, it is not only okay to wait, but beneficial. So again, remember to explain that real meaningful sex is between two people who love each other and have a real commitment, preferably in marriage.
- Although you always hope for a girl to wait to have sex, I strongly believe in teaching about condoms and other protection. There are simply too many diseases and unwanted pregnancies in the world today not to fully educate her. As you may already know, the pill certainly does not protect one from disease.
- Provide her with a safe emotional environment. I know these situations or talks can provoke strong reactions, especially from a dad trying to protect and keep his daughter safe. This is not the time to yell, scream, judge, and preach. Rather it is the time to build trust so she will come to you again. However, this also does not mean a dad should be weak and that he shouldn't express his opinion, because he must. A dad shouldn't jump to conclusions about what she is doing, what she wants to do, or about what she is thinking and feeling. If a dad does that, he shuts down communication.
- Teach her to *never* have sex to hold onto to a boy or win a boy over. So many girls do this (take it from a guy who used to be a teenager) and they usually fail. Explain to her that peer pressure, being curious, and the desire to fit in like other students is not a good reason to have sex. In fact, it is a bad reason to have sex. Explain the contradiction of having to look beautiful, but not having sex. In other words, it is okay to look your best to help feel your best which may attract people to them, but attracting people to you does not necessarily mean they are the right person for any kind of relationship, let alone a sexual one.

- Nearly half of the teenagers in high school will have sex before they graduate. Who do you wish to teach them, you or her friends? I strongly believe that while a mom is great for teaching her about her period and bra sizes, dads have to play a serious, if not the main role in teaching her about sex. Why? Because he knows about teenage boys because he once was one and he knows all the tricks that may come along.
- A dad can and should teach his daughter about what should happen on a date and how a boy should treat her—holding the car and restaurant door open, pulling out her chair, and the little things that show respect. If she is not given respect, he is likely there only for sex. So a dad should ask about how a potential suitor treats her and the kind of manners he has.
- Help her to avoid over-generalizations that lead to bad choices. She is likely thinking, "he loves me," or "he thinks (or says) I am beautiful." So she feels it would be okay to reward these sentiments with sex or she wants to be reciprocal with sex as a reward for making her feel good about herself. She needs to understand that a guy will say what she wants to hear to get sex. Maybe not always, but many times.
- When all else fails, let me ask you dad: do you own a shotgun? Ha! (Just kidding.)

In conclusion, a dad should use the gut instincts of both himself and others (including her friends) to gauge his daughter's behavior, especially when it comes time to date. I also honestly believe that during the teenage years, you don't want your daughter to get too attached to any one boy. That's because this simply leads to early heartache and a higher risk of premature sex and pregnancy. Some daughters who fall head over heels with a boy may eventually end up pregnant to keep him around. That doesn't mean, however, you should keep a boy away who treats your daughter with genuine respect. You wouldn't want to push the nice guy away thinking she is spending too much time with him only to push her into the arms of a bad boy. After all, the grass is not always greener on the other side of the fence and in fact, that grass may be filled with snakes.

Another good point to be made is that I believe a dad should tell a boy when he first meets him to leave his daughter like he found her. In other words, make sure he knows they are out on a date and not a sexual romp. In fact, this is the approach my own dad used with my sister. It plants the seed that dad has been around the block himself once or twice. This leads me to another point: don't let your kids get too isolated in your own house either. You don't want to hover over your daughter and their friends, but let your presence be known in the background at those parties or events where you can sense it has the potential to get out of hand. Some kids will even appreciate this as they don't have to deal with the peer pressure of keeping up with everyone else and doing something they might regret. Then finally, and I mentioned this before and cannot emphasize it enough, observe her behavior, dress, friends, how she talks to her friends, what her friends say back to her. Listen to your gut about anything that doesn't seem right to you.

**The Dating Secret Summary:** The keys here are basic: dating before the age of 16 is not recommended. A dad should meet anyone she dates before they start dating. Make sure the boys she dates are respectful long before the actual date, if possible. Setting a curfew is a great idea. Allow her to call you and come get her with no questions asked if she gets stuck on a date or in a bad situation with friends. Get to know her friends and what they are talking about. Educate her on peer pressure, the desires of the boys she meets, and finally talk about sex itself. These things will help her during those rough teenage years and shape her future dating decisions as a woman.

CHAPTER TEN

# THE HANDLING SEX SECRET

*"If passion drives you, let reason hold the reins."*
–Benjamin Franklin

Now that the parameters for dating have been set, the sex issue must be looked at in more detail. The not too exaggerated truth is that it might be easier to stop a wave crashing to the shore than to control the raging hormones of teenagers. This creates another dilemma for parents to deal with. The real problem here, according to most studies, is that the younger a girl has sex, the more damaging it can be and often is. This is compounded by the fact that it becomes hard to regulate sex in a teenager when a parent is often having sex with their spouse. As we have learned so far, good parenting in most things relates to modeling parent behavior. A parent may not smoke, drink, or do drugs, so not indulging in those vices may make sense to a teen. However, how do you tell a teen to wait when you are having sex yourself? Let's face it, sex can feel really satisfying. How does that old joke go? "The worse sex I ever had was still pretty good." In fact, sex is not just for procreation, but part of the pleasure God intended for us to enjoy and share. Therefore, it must be looked at as a gift to be shared with the right person at the right time.

Let's get back to the age issue and the problem with having sex too early in one's life. Did you know that early sex is linked to depression and high-risk behaviors? In fact, when it happens too early in a girl's life, instead of finding pleasure, it almost becomes a desperate attempt to find love and acceptance for a daughter that she is lacking in other relationships. This is especially true if she has sex before she is emotionally ready to do so. Some girls may appear physically ready to have sex, but emotionally, they are definitely not ready, whether they realize this or not.

Sadly, the pressure to have sex can be reinforced by boys who are trying to attain their own conquest and explore their own sexuality as well. To achieve this end, boys will tell girls that they are loved, pretty, have great bodies, and give them other compliments so they can achieve their "goal" of having sex. Now, before I beat up on the desires of teenage boys, we should remember that some compliments are genuine. They may think they really love a girl or think she is beautiful, but for the most part, in terms of many compliments being genuine: not so much. But it comes down to that person—who he is? Is he believable? Ah yes, the ongoing battle for female genitalia; I remember it well myself because I once spent time as a teen, believe it or not. I will say this: for most teenage boys, the goal of having sex for pure pleasure reigns supreme. A boy will say almost anything to achieve his desires. How do I know that? I did it myself. I once told a girl I was going in the military and that I might die and never see her again. Now, all that was true (well, I didn't expect to die unless I fell off a boat) but, as you might guess, it worked like a charm. So when I hear a girl say someone is a "nice guy," I remember I was called that as well despite various sexual conquests. Let it be said, sex and pleasure are powerful drugs.

However, sex can go beyond just pleasure. It can be an attempt to achieve acceptance for both sexes, not only for themselves and from their partner, but from their peers who often are aware of what is going on with their friends. Achieving these factors of acceptance can be both a conscious and unconscious goal. When both sexes succeed and reach this "goal," it can say to their inner mind, "Someone likes me and desires me," and "I am worthy of being loved" (if only for short time.) However without a true and continual emotional connection between both people involved in having sex with each other, reaching that goal can be fleeting, confusing, and eventually a disappointing event, especially from the girls perspective. So this desire to be accepted by any male can be delayed if her dad is in the home guiding her, hugging her, and showing basic affection. It is when dad is not around that a girl can take affection too far into sex with a boy before she is ready and end up with damaging consequences. So it can be said that many girls use affection for acceptance, but may feel they have to give more physically of themselves to a boyfriend than they normally would otherwise if dad was around giving simple hugs and kisses.

Knowing that a daughter is looking for acceptance and reassurance, it becomes important for a dad to help guide and instruct her to guard her heart and body during those difficult teen years so that she can make good choices. She must then take this information with her so she can make even more solid choices as she gets older and blossoms into a woman. It is unrealistic to believe a girl can make horrible choices with sex and boys as a teen and suddenly start making great choices as a woman simply because the calendar says she is a little bit older. I believe this process of good choices begins by dad (who has been through this before and knows what boys are thinking) explaining to his daughter that sex is not a physical activity for acceptance, but rather a way to express love and caring to another person that should be reciprocated at the same level by the other person involved. This also means there should be a relationship where there is a commitment of mutual feelings beyond the physical realm and that a couple is expressing a gift of caring about each other on a deeper level. The girl is not merely a receptacle for built-up sexual frustration by hormone-driven boys and loved-starved girls wanting affection because they feel alone. If this is explained to a girl before she dates, it at least makes her more aware of the emotional connection and commitment that should be present before she engages in sex and will perhaps delay sex or make her choose more carefully who she has sex with. This may seem like a small victory, but every victory counts. You never know when a girl will soak up this advice like a sponge and make some good choices regarding her body and mind. Perhaps she will wait until she is an adult or even until she is married to have sex. Now wouldn't that be something? Waiting until you are married still has a romantic appeal to many, but it is hard to understand that when you are teen and your circle of peers are having sex. In other words, a daughter needs guidance and dad needs to show her the way.

Another important key to understand is that almost every human being desires human touch and will seek it out from both appropriate and even inappropriate places. This is where a dad comes into play. Appropriate touch in the form of hugs and kisses from dad are an important way to convey love to his daughter and show acceptance. When a daughter feels accepted and loved, it often delays her need to find this acceptance and love in all the wrong places or at too early of an age. When her dad is absent or doesn't show affection, a daughter will seek out human touch from people that can harm her or make her feel used and unworthy of future love and acceptance. It can also make her feel tainted, and negatively affect her self-esteem.

Although there are girls and eventually women who want sex just for sex sake and desire it as much as any man, for the most part, a girl will delay these needs in her teen years if she is accepted, loved, and given appropriate affection from her dad. In other words, teen boys may want more sex, but a teen girl may desire more affection and acceptance and can get by on that. That's why a dad needs to show affection and hug and kiss his daughter on a regular basis; to help delay inappropriate touch and desires that may be absent in her life if dad is not around. Also, as I explained earlier, depending on the boy she dates, a dad can express how a boy thinks at the same time. It should be explained that while not every teenage boy has illicit intentions in mind and they can also sometimes mistake sex for acceptance, for the most part, boys have sex on the brain for the sake of having sex. There can be an overwhelming urge for a boy to have a sexual release regardless of who gets hurt and the emotions involved. Therefore, it is far better early on that physical acceptance and appropriate affection comes from a dad rather than a boy who doesn't have the right intentions. Dads, hug and kiss your daughters!

To explore this further, girls often have sex early because they often subconsciously lack physical contact, affection, and guidance from their dads, or worse yet, their dads are not even in their lives. This should be avoided at all costs if possible. Moms of daughters need to make sure that dads are involved even if they live separately from each other because of divorce. This is not the time to be competitive with each other as parents. Let me say it again until it becomes ingrained in your mind: always love your children more than you hate your ex. In the end, you will get more love and respect from your children for doing so and you will feel good about yourself if you take the high road with the other parent.

Let's get back to the subject. For a dad, it comes down to this: despite what a daughter may see on television or hear from her friends, the two main goals he should keep in mind that his daughter needs to understand are that love and sex go together and are not different entities in mind or body, and it benefits her to delay sex as long as possible. If a dad or any parent can achieve these two goals, it almost always results in more mature thinking and better decisions by his daughter as time passes by.

Unfortunately, some girls may not readily want to follow a parent's advice. They may even make the mistake of correlating being cool, desirable, or being an adult with having sex early. But the sad fact is: these girls are disappointed time after time. Also, in losing their virginity early, some girls lose self-respect especially since early sex is often without the true intimacy, romance, love, or commitment one would need during this time of life. In addition, she can be ostracized by school friends depending on what the prevailing attitude toward sex is by the group. They may also brutalize her by calling her a slut or a whore and spread rumors about her. This is pretty harsh treatment when you realize someone is just trying to seek acceptance or find love, even if it just fleeting puppy love.

Take "Josie's" story, for instance:

> A few of my friends had boyfriends and I was really feeling the pressure to have one as well. I met this guy who was both popular and considered a lot of fun. We went out on a few dates and I was confident I could control how far it went. There was some kissing and petting involved in our dates, but it didn't take too

long to figure out this was not the right guy for me. I knew he wasn't someone I would always be with, but we still went out. Eventually, we went to a party together and people were getting drunk. I had a few drinks myself and was feeling pretty good. At the end of the night after many people left, some couples paired off in different rooms and so did I with my boyfriend. I figured we would kiss and cuddle like we had before and then call it a night. However, I quickly realized my boyfriend wanted more and my inhibitions were at the point to where I eventually gave in. He didn't even have a condom with him. He didn't last long and the sex was over before it even started in my mind. As you might expect, I didn't have time to get excited, let alone have an orgasm. I was laying there thinking, "That's it?" Then he rolled over and passed out. My thinking then switched to how I was going to get home. However, that's not even close to the worst part. I ended up with two "gifts" from this bad experience. First, I became pregnant. Yeah, pregnant at 16 with a guy I wasn't even crazy about. The second gift was a sexually transmitted disease called Chlamydia. I thought to myself, "Great. Just great. How stupid can I be?"

For Josie and many other teens, they learn the hard way. Having a daughter is tough for any parent at this tender age. So what can you do? Let me reemphasize those main points again before we move on. Again we know that the two main goals are to delay sex as long as possible in your daughter and explain to her that love and sex go together. However, let me reassure you that there are a few others things that can help. For instance, for those parents who don't think their children are listening, there may be some good news. Research indicates that kids who feel their parents don't want them to have sex are less likely to have sex. Isn't that interesting? Certainly that is not always the case, but if you have built up a good relationship with your daughter and you make your feelings known, that could be a key factor in preventing negative circumstances from happening. This is a much better approach as a parent than saying you know sex is going to happen anyway and throwing condoms to them. These are the same or similar type of parents who think their kids are going to drink so they might as well throw them a party at their house. This seems like a defeatist attitude to me.

Next, a dad must also explain the potential nasty bugs and consequences that can come from sex. Although it can be awkward, you must talk about STDs, HIV, pregnancy, cervical cancer, the higher rates of both depression and STDs that are all related to early sexual activity, and did I mention the sexual desire of the average teenage boy? Oh, I think I did! In all seriousness, never be afraid to talk to your daughters about sex. They are often confused about some aspects although they may say they know all about it to avoid talking about it. Don't let that happen. If it gets awkward, bring your sense of humor to the discussion to get your points across.

There are some daughters who actually want to save themselves for marriage. Another idea to help a daughter in this desire—though it may seem cheesy to some—is to get her an abstinence ring or bracelet. It may not seem like a viable solution for everyone who has the same goal, but it does give a daughter something to live up to. If you feel you have to live up to something, the tendency is that you will give a good effort to live up to that expectation. Even if it does not work all the way to marriage, it will often help put off sex for a while, which is the real key here. You are essentially buying time and waiting for the maturity process to kick in. Therefore this can be a very effective tool, especially when there is good communication between a daughter and her parents, specifically her dad. These rings and bracelets often say things like "True Love Waits" and in that sense, it is not cheesy at all. Preaching abstinence is one reminder of the expectations you have for her and that she should save herself for someone special. This ends up building her self-worth, self-esteem, and strength. Sure, abstinence isn't going to work for everyone. But as I said earlier, even if it delays the beginning of sex, you are ahead of the game.

Finally, a dad doesn't need to be an expert on this subject. He just needs the ability to talk about how early sex may negatively affect future choices, her future marriage, or her choice in a husband. At the same time, he can reinforce the point that waiting for her wedding day can be a special thing to do. Even if she doesn't wait until marriage to have sex, the message is clear that sex is for someone special and she should wait to share that gift. At this point, at least a dad has given her a choice and ideas to think about in this vital area of her life. So, two questions arise here: when is the best time to begin to talk to a daughter about sex? When should the bulk of this information be given to a daughter? These are easily answered by saying that the process of educating a daughter begins from an early age and continues as she ages, but the bulk of the information should be given to her in her early teen years when she can grasp it.

From the time she is a little girl, her parents need to teach her to respect her body and that no one but doctors and her parents can see her private parts. Why? Besides being proper, if you teach a girl modesty and respect for her body as a young girl, this will carry over as well as she gets older. Again, it is not about being prudish and creating frigid wives in the future. It is about getting a girl to respect herself and her body. Trust me; there are some girls who are going to do what they want no matter what. But is that what you want for your daughter? Always remember that it is about giving a daughter solid information and trying to delay sex as long as possible so good decisions can be made pertaining to all aspects of her intimate relationships and so that sex can be enjoyed as it was intended to be later on as an adult (or at least until she gets older).

Speaking of enjoying sex, I don't want anyone to get the wrong idea; no one here is against sex, especially since it is very important in the lives of most people. However, what I am saying is that it just needs to be the right circumstances or it can become a negative thing for many women and even some men in their lives. In fact, someday I will write another book for adult daughters that will show the importance of actually having sex instead of not having sex and that sex is actually vital for keeping marriages together, which can seem like the opposite of delaying sex in a teen. So just remember this is an important distinction to make: sex is and can be a great thing, but not until one is physically, mentally, and emotionally ready and committed to someone who is equally committed to them. In fact, if the other person is married to them, this would be an ideal situation in giving to someone who cares about you as you care for them.

The Handling Sex Secret Summary: While sex is used for acceptance by both sexes, a dad must help try to delay the sexual activity of his daughter until she is old enough to make more mature emotional, mental, and physical choices that will not harm her or ruin her ability to enjoy sex as an adult. A dad also needs to remind her that love, commitment, and sex all go together if she wants to be truly happy. Otherwise a relationship will feel fragmented and unfulfilling. For most women to be happy, they need more than sex. They need love and commitment and this process begins in the early years.

CHAPTER ELEVEN

# THE BODY IMAGE SECRET

*"It is characteristic of wisdom not to do desperate things."*
–Henry David Thoreau

One of the biggest problems that a dad or any parent faces today is the early sexualization of his daughter in society which translates into a societal expectation of girls and women to conform to an unrealistic standard of physical beauty. This internalized pressure further creates and transfers into an obsession with body image by the female affected. When this happens, a daughter desperately tries to reflect back on what she thinks society wants her to be, thus beginning this vicious cycle. Also notice I said the "female affected" and not the teen affected. Why? Because body image issues can affect the female psyche her entire life and she may never feel comfortable with her body. Guess what the topper is: society contributes to this illogical thinking.

Ironically, one of the biggest predictors of this damage from body image issues in a girl's life is a lack of a present father, especially a biological father. Fathers help reassure a daughter that she is loved unconditionally and accepted whatever her physical condition is. She is accepted by the first male in her life for who she is and not what she looks like. Likewise, daughters look to their dads as knowledgeable and experienced in life so they are apt to accept his reassurance and not continually obsess over smaller things since she is unconditionally made to feel worthy as a human being. Unfortunately, in a society where people are getting divorced at the drop of a hat for real or imagined events, it often puts a father on the outside looking in as the number of single-parent families sadly grows in a "me first" generation. This has not only the potential to produce horrific consequences, it actually does produce adverse effects for many girls and women who attempt to please by presenting themselves to society by their looks, beauty, and body alone, while forgetting or deemphasizing the importance of the core of who she is as a person.

The sexual bombardment of young girls' minds starts early in life. In fact, it seems like as early as girls can walk, at least some of them are entered into beauty pageants. This may not seem like a huge matter, but from an early, formative age, girls that are entered into pageants are taught to rely on looks, superficial beauty, and their body as major factors in terms of gaining acceptance from others. In reality, this is not really acceptance at all because it is only skin deep. In addition, if you can live with the notion of child-like curiosity theory and think it's okay because these girls want to be there or want to dress up, then why does it seem like more often than not, the parents are living vicariously through their children and that it is the parent that cares more about winning and losing? For me, it is often heart-breaking to witness a mom throw a fit because the trophy a child wins (and most of them win something anyway) is not the trophy the mom wants or expects. This subsequently transfers the disappointment to the child which often leaves them in tears feeling like they have failed in life.

To make matters worse, this sexualization of girls is prevalent throughout society and is far more insidious than just pageants. In fact, its mixed messages take many forms. Some of these sources include magazines, ads by various means, books, commercials, social media, television programs, video games, clothing stores, cosmetics aisles, weight loss diets, even cookies that supposedly make your breasts grow! Plus the message sent to every girl and woman is therefore clear: conform and try to look like a model or be found unacceptable. How is that for pressure?

Another major problem in this millennium is the race to look like Barbie or another unrealistic female image as girls become young women. This is the time period when plastic surgery, collagen and Botox injections, liposuction, nose jobs, breast jobs, and other ways to radically change the way one looks is sweeping across the nation. Sadly, the underlying message is almost always, "You are not good enough the way you are." The deeper meaning being sent is that you need to get something done to fit in with everyone else.

Another sad aspect related to body image is that women perceive these extreme ideals as what men really want and that is certainly not the case. Sure, from a visual standpoint, a large bosom can be attractive. But that is not necessarily what men want, especially if the parts are plastic or not real. Let me explain this further with a comparison. A huge male bodybuilder may be attractive to some females. They may admire his muscularity, power, symmetry, and definition. However, in most studies, women respond to and actually prefer a thinner physique that is perhaps defined with a well-shaped rear, not necessarily someone who is too big or bulky and perhaps on steroids. (But that's another story.) Ironically, the type of lean physique that women respond to and prefer is also close to what men prefer in a female: someone with a thin to medium build and a well-shaped rear, but no excessive or fake parts.

You will get exceptions here, however. For instance, you can have some women addicted to bodybuilders or men who prefer very large breasts. However, for the most part, both genders prefer someone in shape with a lean build. A man can still be a "breast man" and like to look at larger breasts, but still like and actually prefer an average and even a smaller bosom in a relationship. If more women actually knew they would be accepted for a more normal and average look by the men they meet, perhaps they would think twice before going to these physical extremes.

The bombardment of society's jaded expectations and lack of information creates much of this internalized pressure and insecurity in a female, resulting in the desire to have bigger breasts and other procedures done to meet them. It is this very insecurity of a girl or woman not measuring up in her mind or thinking this what men want that begins this pilgrimage to be more attractive to them. However, this look is superficial and fleeting without substance. General physical attractiveness is important and will get you in the door, as most studies have shown. But it won't keep you around. In fact, if a person's personality or attitude is bad, who is going to want this girl or woman around? Therefore, physical attractiveness will only take you so far in any relationship in life.

As I mentioned earlier, there is no question that some men are intrigued by and actually like the Barbie lookalike. But in real life, most men really do prefer women who are simply in shape especially if that shape is not the exaggerated look of huge breasts, huge lips, a face pulled taut, and bleached-blonde hair. To add another level to this conversation, men also don't prefer someone that appears to be high maintenance physically; someone looking for the next expensive procedure that they simply must have. Oh, and while I am here: high maintenance in other areas of someone's life is a turnoff as well. But that is another story.

Going back to physical beauty: a good share of males can be simply turned off by women who go to extremes or have unnecessary procedures because so many of these women look alike and because there is a bit of fakeness to it. However, let me say this clearly: I am not against anyone who really feels they need to get some work done on their bodies or faces if they believe it will help them in terms of appearance or self-esteem or so they can feel better about themselves and they don't overdo it. Some people do have disfigurements or nose issues that can be corrected to make them feel better and to enhance their confidence. However, as we have witnessed too often, from the average person to the famous movie and music stars, many have been disfigured by doing too many enhancements and procedures because it can be addictive. Also, it can create not just cosmetic problems, but issues with silicone implants leaking can create internal havoc.

So remember, in terms of procedures, less is more if you have to get something done. Again, the key is to make sure this body and facial work is done for the right reason. Even when someone thinks it is, often times, it is not. That's why it is important to consult family and friends to get feedback from them as well, which includes getting an opinion from someone you trust. Among the wrong reasons to get work done would be to compete with other people to fit in, for a job (yes even to be a stripper), or to attract others superficially—doing it for someone other than themselves. The real "surgery" I would suggest as an alternative is to find internal beauty in themselves and to take time to "dissect" who they really are and who they really want to be. This is a surefire way to attract the right people (and right men) into their lives. The good news here for girls becoming women is that most men—at least the men you should be seeking—prefer a natural and normal appearance with an abundance of inner beauty to go along with it. That's a good look!

In addition, women need to understand that Hollywood and the porn industry are not the real world for modeling what the rest of the world should look like. These are industries that require or create a certain look to create a fantasy. While men are the biggest purveyors of porn, women can't totally blame men for this image obsession with these certain looks because, as the old adage goes, "women tend to dress for women." In other words, women are competitive with other women in terms of how they look in all aspects—body, face, hair style, and what they wear. They try to keep up with them in terms of the latest fashion trends, including plastic surgery and those unrealistic looks from porn and Hollywood. Therefore, women tend to follow the unrealistic or fantasy look when they should just create the look that feels comfortable to them and reinforces who they are in their everyday life. I will, however, leave the subject of role-playing and fantasy looks in your own intimate relationships up to you as adults.

So where do fathers come in? Dads play a unique role in protecting their daughter from becoming over-sexualized by first accepting them as they are. A daughter will pick up cues from her father on his attitude toward women. For example, does a father overemphasize weight loss beyond normal health reasons? Does he emphasize looking a certain way that uses plastic surgery? Does he appreciate natural beauty or does he like and talk about a fantasy look? Does he look at porn or provocative magazines? Is the father involved in making sure that his daughter is not dressing in an overtly sexual way to attract the wrong attention or conform to 'what everyone else is doing? Does he prefer or pressure his wife or daughter into losing weight or even to have plastic surgery beyond reasons of their health? These are all cues and triggers to how a daughter will react and how she feels about her own body image.

You see, there is an even bigger problem at work here as well. When trying to conform and finally caving into an over-sexualized society of fantasy look and dress, there can be dire consequences like early promiscuity, the potential for sexual assaults, early or teen pregnancy, rape, and other crimes related to girls seeking to attract males in all the wrong places for all the wrong reasons. This problem is originally created by this overly-sexualized society that people are trying to conform to. It creates a problem where there should be less of an issue. Even if we say it doesn't matter how a girl looks or what she wears and it shouldn't create a problem, is that realistic? Of course it isn't. Because of that, fathers need to be involved in their daughter's lives and again, moms need to make sure that happens and dad is around. It has to be conveyed from dad because this is where daughters are wondering what males are thinking, especially their own fathers. There are no substitutions and moms cannot effectively carry this role because mom may be dressing for other women or creating her own look based on society and a daughter really needs more in-depth reasoning ingrained into her soul. Why? A daughter may listen to her mother, but it may go in one ear and out the other if not congruent with what her dad says, how he acts, and how he is observed to behave in regards to women. This is what she is really looking at because down the line, she may end up with someone like her father or feel her father's beliefs about women are what she should strive to be as she goes looking for a mate of her own. The most important thing to remember is that throughout her life, first as a girl, and then subsequently a woman, various outcomes (whether positive or negative) are tied to her father. There is no getting around it.

So what else can a father do to help this situation? The key here is to focus more on her inner beauty than her outer beauty, which I admit, isn't the easiest thing to do. This is because human nature arises and people want to talk about what they see rather than who someone may be. It doesn't hurt to compliment a daughter's outer beauty on occasion so a daughter is both comfortable and reassured with the way she looks. After all, for many girls and women who have listened to hundreds of compliments (especially the average girl or woman), they may actually feel like they are hearing a compliment for the first time because of ongoing societal pressure and personal insecurity. It's especially important that everybody, especially girls, look good and feel good about themselves. This can often present a challenge when you remember they are being bombarded with cover girl comparisons and peer pressure. But if you can tap into that inner beauty, it opens up a whole new secret to success in her life.

There is a big difference between a girl feeling pretty or confident about her appearance and wanting to make small changes with fashion and make-up and a girl obsessing about exercise, diets, or cosmetic surgeries. One way to lessen this obsession with skin-deep beauty is for dad to work on building a girl's self-esteem and self-worth. This helps lessen the preoccupation with looks or at least helps keep it in perspective. One of the best ways to do that is to understand that a girl's body image is closely associated with how her father perceives and talks about women and how he nurture's his daughter's self-esteem. I touched on this earlier: if her dad often talks about women in an overtly physical way, enjoys women who flaunt their bodies, looks at naked women in magazines or on porn sites, then it may signal to his daughter that by doing the same thing, she can win male approval through physical appeal rather than compatibility and personality. Contrast that with a dad that shows affection to the women in his life and appreciates their beauty in a respectful way that recognizes good taste and modesty, and who also appreciates women that present themselves that way, then you have a situation that builds lasting self-worth in this girl or woman. In this latter case, he respects women for who they are. This is an important lesson that his daughter will observe and make mental notes of as she moves through her life.

Another area where fathers can help is in the prevention of eating disorders. While we have established that a dad can and should tell his daughter she is beautiful both inside and out, she needs to have proper information if she plans to work in the glamour industry. She needs to know the flood of unreality that awaits any girl trying to get work as a model in magazines, commercials, movies, and on television. Another issue is that a girl may be starving herself or have unhealthy eating habits but not realize that many times, model photos are airbrushed or photo-shopped to meet an unrealistic standard.

How prevalent are these eating disorders and body image issues? It is estimated that four out of five women are unhappy with their bodies and this can cause many issues with food. This often means that the more they eat, the more stress develops over the fear of gaining weight. This then becomes a vicious cycle because the unhappier they are with their bodies, the more they may eat. It can also lead go in the opposite direction of not eating enough (chronic under-eating) or starving themselves. If these abnormal conditions or relationships with food are allowed to continue over time, it can lead to even more serious conditions like obesity, bulimia, or anorexia.

A condition like obesity can lead to even more problems. For example, chubby kids are often picked on, dismissed, made fun of, and in short, bullied. In fact, being overweight can increase bullying by 63 percent. Therefore, the synergistic combination of being both overweight and bullied can further increase the already simmering anger in a victim or target. This is also complicated by being emotionally overwhelmed by the situation and puts a person at a nutritional risk as they may desperately try to deal with their situation through weight loss extremes. In other words, this emotional upheaval is often followed by desperate attempts to diet or lose weight in an unhealthy way through fad diets or near starvation. To make matters worse, these weight loss results usually are fleeting or fail, often with the result being that any weight that is lost is often regained and then some. Also, it stands to reason that without a true lifestyle change, these attempts may be futile or at best, a form of yo-yo dieting.

Losing weight doesn't fix the low self-esteem, depression, anxiety, troubled relationships, peer pressure, and stress in a daughter's life. In fact, some people claim they still feel fat on the inside despite substantial external weight loss. If the mind doesn't catch up with the body in terms of lifestyle, self-esteem, and psychological acceptance of who they deserve and desire to be, they will gain the weight back or at least a large portion of it. This is why you often hear the familiar adage that diets don't work. Simply put, all weight loss is connected to the mind.

Therefore, fathers can make a huge difference in developing a daughter's positive body image and helping prevent eating disorders by developing a strong emotional bond with her. This comes from real listening, asking questions, expressing feelings, monitoring behavior, showing an interest in her and what she does, spending quality time with her, speaking your mind (even a little debate will bring security to her life), consistently enforcing rules (rules are nothing without follow through) and finally, building her self-esteem by focusing on who she is as a person with some sincere exterior compliments that all girls and women like to hear.

**The Body Image Secret Summary:** Fathers play an important role in positive body image issues by getting their daughter to focus on who she is as a person and by deftly mixing in some exterior beauty compliments. A daughter should be taught not to compare herself to the unrealistic expectations that many girls and women have of superficial beauty which often lead to poor eating habits and eating disorders. A father's view of women and their bodies can also make a huge impact on his daughter. If his view is a healthy one, a daughter will take her cue from him and often feel the same way and present herself in a way that helps her respect herself. While there is nothing wrong with desiring to be beautiful and have a great body, it should be kept in the perspective of being healthy.

CHAPTER TWELVE

# FOCUS ON HER IDEALS SECRET

"A people that values its privileges above its
principles soon loses both."
–Dwight D. Eisenhower

Among the most important qualities any daughter can develop is to become what I call, the "optimal to ideal self." Optimal is the best we can become realistically, while ideal is the most perfect person we could hope to achieve. This is a "self" that others respect but more importantly, an internal persona or person that a daughter would honestly respect herself. Every day in today's society, we see examples of girls or women we don't want our daughters to become. We all know the type: the girls or subsequently the women with selfish traits or behaviors that are always somewhere between focused and obsessed on the acquisition of material possessions, who lack empathy for others, or someone who simply isn't fun to be around based on their attitude or the way they treat others. When these negative traits are presented excessively (and someone can have a varied percentage of some or all of these traits), it has the ability to severely damage the potential life every girl and subsequently every woman is entitled to have.

Worse yet, some of these women want to change but are unable to do so and wind up in a vicious cycle of chasing their own tail as they keep stepping on the toes of those closest to them. Even though they may momentarily apologize, they will still eventually start this vicious cycle over from the top and continue hurting themselves and others. To top it off, they may not have any remorse, they may feel bad for a moment, but that usually is a fleeting feeling as they have no real regard that they are hurting someone and have become toxic to themselves and to other people. To compound the problem, many sadly think they are doing fine and have no problems mistreating people or believing their next purchase will make them happy. The reality is that they are empty inside and nobody wants to be around them.

Fathers play a critical role in the area of getting a daughter to be her ideal self. In fact, dads are the mentors that a daughter will look to both consciously and unconsciously and therefore end up developing similar traits that he has internalized himself. How does this happen? Besides the unconscious mind doing its thing, just by being around her dad, a girl will closely observe him to see his reactions, attitudes, and actions in the way he treats people, how he treats himself, and in the perspective he puts on personal possessions. Sure, she will look to mom as well to see these same things, but her dad's characteristics in these areas have a lasting impact on who she may and will become. This is because of the innate father-daughter and mother-son connection links to success. This means, as you may have surmised, that a daughter is highly connected to her father in terms of success and failure.

When a daughter can adapt these positive traits to her own character or replace negative traits that her dad might have with positive traits of her own, people will trust her. She'll understand that while having some personal possessions makes life easier, she is not ruled by keeping up with the Jones or Smith families. When a person is not preoccupied with stuff, life becomes easier and it is the little things, like human interaction, that become more important. When this happens, they can focus on who they are becoming and what they want to do, not on what they are accumulating.

I should note here that I am not talking about an issue like hoarding—a condition with a psychiatric/mental disorder component that is often attached to traumatic loss and that should be dealt with by professionals. Nor am I talking about earning or inheriting wealth. Rather, it's the inability to realize that buying their fiftieth pair of shoes will not bring them out of a depression or bring a lasting change of happiness. That mom not cooking her favorite brownies is not the end of the world. That a fiancée who wants to spend a little less on an engagement ring is not suddenly unlovable and that a sales lady is not a goofball because the dress she wanted is no longer in the store and only available online. It is also the inability to realize that temporarily yelling or screaming at someone over some minor event can drastically change the way people see her and feel about her as a person. In some cases, it is the inability to understand that others need compassion, kindness, empathy, sympathy, and a little attention as well. When it becomes a one-sided "it's all about me" sideshow, it is no longer a relationship. It becomes a job for the person not getting even the basic courtesies returned.

In fact, even if these things that someone feels they must have are achieved, it would only be a temporary happiness by simply fulfilling immediate gratification or impulsive urges. It is like eating a bowl of chocolate ice cream and saying to yourself, "That was great. Now what?" The satisfaction doesn't last and the problems remain. In the meantime, this type of daughter becomes so irritable and unattractive to others along the way to achieve these conquests that they don't realize what appears to be a simple indulgence to them is irritating and stepping on toes to others. This is because of the way they do it, how they ask for something to be done, or simply how they treat the people around them during the process. These simple misunderstandings can then lead to a complex and unhappy relationship with someone, especially if it is repeatedly done. You would think that with enough misunderstandings, a person behaving like this would get the picture, but this usually does not happen. They blame others for not understanding their needs and wants and become viewed as toxic by all those around them.

However, with the right perspective and attitude when situations arise in her life, she will be more readily accepted, trusted, and she'll look like a leader as opposed to a spoiled brat. This can be a key component in all relationships and success in life. This positive perspective is modeled from dad to daughter. This also helps dad's perspective. He wants to feel that he is giving or appealing to the appreciative princess in his daughter and not to a continual spoiled rotten brat who ends up being the next bridezilla or worse. Life is about a balance of give and take. It is not all about giving until you become a doormat, nor is it always about taking and being selfish. Who wants to be treated poorly all the time? Who wants to be around materialistic people who have no values or sense of fair play and justice? Who wants to be around someone with no compassion for others because they are caught up in their own little world and it's all about them? Not I, nor should you. Therefore, it's important that a dad build the ideal self in his daughter so she does not become toxic to herself and others.

Fathers can help daughters understand the line between need and greed and also between wants and needs. When it is someone else's money, it always seems like everything is a need. When it is your own money, you must decide between what you really want and what you need in choosing what to buy for yourself. Dads can help her understand the difference between a want and a need and also put into context for his daughter the understanding that material things are fine to have when put in perspective, but they are not the be-all end-all they are purported to be. In fact, in the last few years, many wealthy people have given up substantial amounts of their estates or wealth to charity or other causes to live the simple life and to feel good internally about their own lives. Why? Most studies have shown that it is giving and not receiving that is the basis for true happiness. Therefore, it is those that give, not those that take, that are usually the people who are truly happy. In fact, it is those people that give back to their community or pay it forward that feel genuinely good about themselves, not those individuals always checking their stock quotes.

Now, a certain amount of money or material things may be important to feel comfortable in life, but when it gets excessive, it can have the opposite effect. Even some lottery winners regret winning because it complicated their lives. Instant wealth changed the dynamics of the relationships they once had with family and friends and in some cases, they felt like they were targets of those wanting a piece of the pie. It is similar in terms of relationships. Treating people with respect earns respect back most of the time because, to put it in layman's terms, if you kick over the beehive, it's hard to get the honey. Sure, not everyone is going to treat you well even when you make the effort to do the same. People are flawed and if you rely on them for happiness, you are going to be disappointed most of your life. You must depend on yourself for your own happiness but that doesn't mean you get to treat people badly. In fact, it's just the opposite; always try to take the high road in dealing with people, forgive others, and move on. Taking the high road and focusing less on possessions are things a dad can teach his daughter.

As I previously mentioned, it's important for a dad to get his daughter to shift any preoccupation on an obsession with "stuff" like the latest car, new shoes, clothes, and other toys, and instead focus on who she is and what her ideals are—her character, standards, relationships, family and friends, ability to give and receive love unconditionally, and the ability to forgive herself and others, with empathy for all. Putting it all together, let's agree on this: while it may be important to be stylish and assertive, it has to be in perspective. If a girl's happiness depends on the purchase of the latest gadget or treating someone badly, insensitively, or aggressively to get what she wants, a dad needs to get involved.

Let's take the case of a girl I will call "Karnie," who I first met as a teenager. When I first laid eyes on her, I was absolutely shocked by her natural beauty, bright smile, kindness, and relaxed and almost shy demeanor. She was hired an as intern where I worked to help wherever she was needed. She enthusiastically did a great job and was well thought of by everyone she worked with. Her model good looks eventually led her to California and I lost track of her for a long time as she pursued her dreams. Years later, I met her again when she had come back to our state to visit some of her family that was still living here. The first things I noticed about her were her physical features. Her breasts were now huge, her lips looked bigger, and her nose was now narrowed and smaller. She looked like she had just come from a cookie cutter-plastic surgeon and I guess to some, she looked like some Playboy fantasy. For me, however, to look at her was sad. The natural beauty was gone and now she looked like everyone else that had a lot of work done.

The worst part, though, was her attitude. She was now acting like a diva, especially toward her boyfriend as she ordered him around. In fact, she seemed annoyed at everyone around her although she flashed me a smile and asked how I was doing. However, something had changed. The girl who was quick to wait on people and help out wherever she could now demanded that people wait on her. To me, she didn't look or act like the unique person she was. I kidded her and asked if she was now a famous movie star. She replied that she was doing some modeling in California. When she went to the bathroom, her boyfriend informed me that her modeling was actually adult films and that her DVDs were for sale if I wanted one. I'm not sure if I was more surprised by the fact that she was doing adult films or that her creepy boyfriend was trying to sell some to me.

Anyway, she later came over and said, "I need to talk to you tomorrow." I said no problem and she stopped by my office the next day without her boyfriend. When she arrived, she plopped down in a chair across from me and smiled brightly.

I said to her, "I haven't seen you in a long time, so California must be good to you?" At this point, the smiled disappeared from her face and light tears cascaded down both cheeks.

"Actually," she said as she forced out a nervous laugh, "it's been somewhat of a nightmare."

I responded with the only thing I could think of at the time, which was, "Why is that?"

She responded by telling me she had planned to go to California to get into modeling to pay for acting lessons and then attempt to become a television or movie star. However, as she further explained, she got detoured and modeling jobs were infrequent so she waited tables and then eventually turned to adult films for easy cash. It was in the adult film industry where she met her current boyfriend. During this time, she said she felt pressure to have plastic surgery and various enhancements to create a certain fantasy on screen. For some reason, she went with it and she made a lot of money. I asked her how her family felt about all this. "My family…" she paused and then looked down before starting again. "My family has always been broken. My mom and dad divorced and mom had a bunch of boyfriends who were all trying to hit on me. My dad wasn't in the house so that created stress on me because we were close. However, I remember him always having a big stack of magazines with naked women in them. Mom's boyfriends were always talking about women in an overtly sexual way. So I guess this is what I thought men admired and so I tried to live up to that fantasy."

"So," I said, "I guess you are saying it is not really working for you?"

"That's an understatement," she added.

I said, "Look, I think the biggest thing to focus on right now is who you are on the inside and who you really want to be, not what others expect of you. You don't have to be famous to be happy and you don't have to change the way you look to make others like you or accept you."

You know, it's funny what people take to heart. Within a year, she had moved back to town, started working as a co-manager of a fine dining restaurant, and although she still had some of the effects of cosmetic procedures, she tried to deemphasize them through modest clothing. Her personality seemed to make the biggest change. She was no longer the shy teenager I first met, which is a good thing. But she was relaxed, comfortable, laughing, and among other things, helpful to others. When I walked into the restaurant for the first time, she ran over, gave me a big hug, kissed me on the cheek, and said, "Thank you!"

I said, "For what?"

She looked me straight in the eye and quietly said, "You know what."

I looked at her and said, "You're welcome. Oh, and welcome home." Both of us locked eyes, smiled, and went on our way. Here's the thing: Karnie needed to understand that who she is internally is way more important than what she needed to appear to be to other people. That a kind, positive, and loving personality would take her farther in life—and in any true relationship with others—than enlarged breasts and inflated lips would. That's because what's on the inside would be more genuine in terms of emotions, real in the sense of being authentic, and long-lasting.

This is why fathers are so important. A dad can teach his daughter to be humble, kind, independent, to love others, to be her own person, and to develop herself as a role model that others look up to, even when mentoring from others sources is available to her or she borrows positive traits from those she admires. In fact, it is her dad that is the irreplaceable x-factor in a daughter's life if she really wants to be all she can be and the data studies back this up. If she becomes who she needs to be on the inside, she not only becomes a model for others to follow, but she can leave the world in a better place than how she found it.

Can you imagine the personal growth acquired when a girl learns that the little things in life are important? That giving is more important to psychological health than getting? That a note, letter, flower, or favor can change someone's day? Think of the power one may have when they as a human being practice respect toward another person and don't dismiss their feelings or put them down. Furthermore, a dad that can help his daughter look at both sides of any debate, helps her grow in wisdom, and enhances the communication skills she'll need through life. In fact, this is a particular skill that enormously helped someone by the name of Abraham Lincoln. Amazingly, as a lawyer, old Abe had the knack of presenting the case against him first before presenting his side of the case. Why? Because he felt it lessened the power of the other side if he conceded some things and took away the opponents thunder. Sure enough, he was often right. Admitting you are not perfect while you mention some of your mistakes will help when constructively dealing with others and their problems. When you admit you are flawed, it builds acceptance and part of building the ideal self is the ability to know and share that you are not perfect.

Let's mention self-esteem next in searching for the ideal self. This is one of the most important aspects in the development of any person, especially for teen girls becoming women. In fact, I could write a whole book on self-esteem as it relates to formulating success for any woman. As I have touched on before, the ideal form of self-esteem in a daughter is fostered not by her being dependent on what she does, her accomplishments, or even her superficial looks. Rather it is based on who she really is deep down inside as a person. It's that mental, emotional, and spiritual being she has to nurture if she is to become her ideal self and attain the ultimate goal of self-actualization. Self-actualization can be defined as a pursuit of the ideal self. This means being able to optimally express one's creativity, spiritual enlightenment, pursuit of knowledge, to give back to society to improve it by continually striving in this positive direction to be better, and ultimately by discovering and becoming who she was meant to be in this world.

Another ideal trait in becoming the ideal self is learning to live with humbleness and humility. Humility is important because it helps a person be accepted by the people around her. However, if a daughter acts superior to other people, she risks being ostracized or isolated from others. Being sincerely humble helps to build longer-lasting, genuine friendships based on simple respect and honesty. People will tend to like her and respect her because she doesn't act like she is better than anyone else or exaggerate her importance. In other words, if you blow your horn too much, you become a blowhard. Let others talk about what you have accomplished in life. Humility also teaches a daughter to love people for who and where they are without critical judgment because many times, people who lack the humble gene are quick to judge others. Imagine the difference between having a daughter who is gracious and thankful and one who is self-centered, self-absorbed, spoiled, arrogant, and never happy with anyone or anything. The difference is striking. Therefore, teaching a daughter to be humble through her life can make all the difference in the world in developing the relationships that lead to success.

Much of what we are discussing when it comes to developing your optimal self comes down to integrity. Integrity is living with sincerity and honesty and being true to a set of values that can't be shaken. It's a way of sticking to your principles by being unyielding like a rock, but being open and flexible enough to at least listen to what others are saying and consider their opinion. It's being rock solid and remembering what is really important in life instead of immediate gratification or trying to hurt someone. So in the end, a dad can and needs to have an important role in the way she thinks and acts in these key areas which ultimately are to her benefit and help raise her expectations for a great life. Think of it this way: who we are not only affects others, it affects us.

The Ideal Secret Summary: The secret here is for a daughter to develop her own ideal self where she learns to respect herself and others. This means getting less focused on material things and discovering the beauty within. The best way to achieve this is by dad setting an example in how he treats others, his values, and how he keeps material things in perspective. However, regardless of what dad teaches and passes to his daughter via observation, action, and words, in the end, she still needs to find the way to live with the important traits of unconditional love, forgiveness, empathy, and humbleness. It also means that a daughter needs to learn that the little things mean a lot in life. Ultimately, the ideal self is a person of sincerity, honesty, and integrity. Show me any person—let alone a daughter—like this, and more often than not I will show you someone who is very successful in life.

CHAPTER THIRTEEN

# THE RESOLVE SECRET

"In the confrontation between the stream and the rock, the stream always wins. Not through strength, but by perseverance."
–H. Jackson Brown Jr.

Resolve is defined as the fixity of purpose. In other words, it's the ability to be fixed on a goal until you achieve it and to overcome adversity when you are being tested in trying to reach this goal. Resolve, therefore, is an important skill to have throughout life if a person wants to reach the goals they have set for themselves. In fact, can you imagine the success in life a daughter might have when a dad provides an example of starting and finishing his own projects, getting things done, and of not giving up, especially when others would? As we all know, most of us face bumps in the road of life and sometimes those bumps can get overwhelming to the point where we want to quit. But quitting, contrasted with the ability to overcome, persist, and reach our goals is no real comparison. In addition, for better or worse, there is a strong correlation between the resolve dad has and uses in his own life and what his daughter tends to acquire from him in exhibiting her own resolve as a result of him becoming an example for her to follow. Therefore, we can say a daughter needs to take a dad's good traits with her through life and find or reinvent the rest through awareness.

Let's face it: life is not easy and a dad must help his daughter bounce back from adversity and fight on via verbal encouragement and by presenting himself as a model battling through his own adversity, issues, and bumps. Children are smart; they will listen to what someone says about what they or someone else should do. However, they will be closely watching to see if what they do actually matches with what they say. A dad can talk all he wants about hanging in there, but if he presents himself as someone who is always quitting or giving up, he is sending mixed messages to his daughter. After all, why shouldn't she quit if he quits? Simply put, there is a stronger resolve and persistence in a daughter if her father is steadfast in overcoming his own trials and tribulations and fights the good fight. She can actually see and feel the determination he has to get things done and she knows from firsthand knowledge that it's not just all talk.

Dad then becomes an example for the notion that if life gives you a bad break, you can overcome and conquer. This is important because some of these things that seemed devastating and long-suffering as a teenager, in the grand scheme of things, are relatively temporary or short-term problems. As adults, we can look back and wonder why we were so upset over a pimple, a wart, the size of our nose, a friend who no longer likes us, a breakup with a boyfriend or girlfriend, or some other thing we perceived as embarrassing or a permanent fatal flaw at the time. The tragic realization is that something perceived as suffering with no end in sight, at least to them, can lead a teenager to drastic solutions like suicide.

When problems come up for his daughter, that should automatically send dad on a fact-finding mission to find out why she might be upset and what is really happening in her life even when it is something a dad perceives in his own mind to be not that upsetting. In these instances, he needs to listen and dig deeper to find out her inner feelings and what she is really trying to say. In fact, because of life experience, there may be times when an issue may seem minor to a parent, but may be very important to her. It's not an easy process and sometimes with teenagers, you have to read between the lines because they are not always forthcoming with information. However, if a dad can lend an ear to listen to her and show acceptance, it can be a big help to his daughter, especially when she is a teen. At this point, it is also important for a dad to share his own personal experience. This gives her a reference point to start from; someone who has gone through similar things can give perspective to the situation and in essence, help her understand that it's not the end of the world. Also, unless a dad expresses his experience, she may not even know he has gone through a similar issue. Dads and daughters need to communicate and find common ground.

Another important fact as it relates to resolve is to realize that there are real concerns and dangers in the world to overcome. For example, if a girl is just texting, she is two times more likely to be using alcohol and three times as likely to be having sex—and that's just texting. What about the scary and damaging effects of rape and realizing the pain doesn't end the day that a trauma like rape occurs? In fact, after a rape, the victim is likely to be 11 times more clinically depressed than the average person, six times more likely to develop a social phobia, and on average, face 15 years of psychological problems. In some severe cases, many more years of turmoil can be added to that number. Sexual violence also crosses both genders and does not just include males as perpetrators. In fact, one study found that lesbians do not escape this issue either, as nearly 30 percent are raped by other women according to a 1992 study on lesbian sexual violence. So it isn't just a heterosexual issue, but it's across the board in a sexualized society. In fact, even those women incarcerated as heterosexuals can turn to homosexual acts including rape to satisfy sexual urges. Sadly, in these latter cases, their victims have no choice.

I make that point for this reason. If a female can do that to another female, let me ask you this: is it any wonder that a dad wants to get his shotgun out when the perceived more sexually aggressive male comes around to court his daughter? Of course not. Dads know that teenage boys have raging hormones and they are smart to want to protect their daughters. Whether male or female, we simply have a sexually aggressive society, especially as more pornography has more readily entered our culture. Don't get the wrong idea from all this information. Sex is a great thing in itself and these may be extreme examples to some, as many girls and women in society are not going to be raped. But my point is that at some junction in everyone's life, the time comes where he/she must face situations—sexual or not—where he/she will feel somewhere between unpleasant and unbearable and yet, overcoming these situations is imperative to being truly happy.

However, for most girls and women, some of the most common obstacles to be faced in life include the following: breakups, body image issues, divorce, loss of a job or losing several jobs over a certain time period, job bullying, financial issues, loss of loved ones, dealing with a disability or chronic disorder, disfigurement, chronic or catastrophic illness or disease, various forms of abuse, giving up on dreams, and poor living conditions, and a host of other problems that may come their way. So guess what: a daughter will be closely looking at her dad to see how he tackles these similar problems himself and how he approaches and deals with other people that have these issues.

So how does a dad help his daughter bounce back and keep going? Besides being an example for overcoming problems and issues, there are other things or steps that would help. First, it's important that a dad give his daughter a bigger purpose and passion for life to keep her going, especially since many issues that seem permanent as a younger person tend to be temporary or their severity and pain seems to lessen considerably over time. Therefore, focusing on the big picture can help a dad keep his daughter looking ahead and looking forward to better things and a better life as opposed to the mundane and trivial things that can pull her down.

Second, a dad needs to make sure that his daughter understands that the only person in this world that can make her happy is the person looking back at her in the mirror and not to depend on others for happiness. It's important for everyone to understand that others can contribute to our happiness, but they can't make us happy. This notion can be foreign to many, especially to girls, teenagers, or even adult women with low self-esteem. I have witnessed projected anger and revenge from people who expected others to save them, take care of them, or pay their way. These are the people you see that have never gone on with their lives, are constantly living in the past trying to screw others over, or are constantly scheming or suing because they are so miserable themselves. These people can never figure out why they are so unhappy and blame others for what could or should have been. They live in a constant state of chaos with negative returns and reactions and they seem surprised because they can never figure out why this happens to them. The reason is rather simple: if you want to live a petty live, expect petty returns.

This is also why breakups can be especially tough for these girls and young women. They wrap their entire lives in a relationship and when it goes wrong or ends, it can seem devastating like the end of the world, especially with limited life experience to go by. At this point, a normal adult may take a few weeks to recover then slowly find their way back to the human race and move past it. However, if this happens to a teenage girl or a woman with low self-esteem, it can put her in a mild to severe depression or even make her suicidal. Therefore, it may be wise to advise her not to get too attached to any one boy. Sure there are stories where two 16-year-olds meet, get married, and live happily ever after. But those are the exceptions and not the rules.

It's also wise to clue her in on the red flags of any relationship, which essentially pertains to how she is treated and respected. In terms of being in a relationship with someone else, she needs to understand you can't change anyone or that change is difficult at best. This is a good rule to keep in mind when chasing those enticing bad boys. In fact, it's always disappointing to a dad to see his daughter or any other woman chase after a bad boy. Why? Because bad boys are almost always people you can never change and are usually emotionally or mentally unavailable, or even sometimes physically unavailable because they are cheating or attached to someone else. They seem like a prize because there is always a challenge involved. Unfortunately, girls are often attracted to boys and then men that are on the living on the edge or have an edge to them. However, when a girl cannot change them, it becomes a relationship wrought with sorrow, regrets, and of course drama. Eventually the girl will try to figure a way out. Therefore, I believe everyone, especially teenage girls and women, should approach all relationships like a potential fire: when it starts out rocky or those red flags appear, stop, look, listen, get on the floor and roll out of there before you get burned.

Of course the difficult thing here is even that with the best information made available, girls and many young women are still drawn to bad boys like a moth to a flame. They are enticed by the initial and then intermittent excitement and danger, but often end up being sad and disappointed long-term and wonder why they are so unhappy. The need to go after bad boys can be summed up by saying it is the psychology of marrying up. They feel that if someone is treating them badly, the other person must be a better person or more important and that is what they deserve to feel good about themselves. If someone is more important or doesn't care about you, they are worthy of pursuing. It meets the female biology of wanting to nurture, save, and change someone, yet being subservient and raptured at other times. In others words, these girls and women are trying to live out a fantasy that has no basis in reality. In fact, when a bad boy becomes or appears to be less available physically, emotionally, and in every other way, they become more attractive to the average female who has lower self-esteem. Meanwhile, the nice guy ends up empty-handed because not only is he not a challenge, he seems desperate. He is the one doing the chasing, bringing flowers and candy, and spending money. But if a girl or woman with low self-esteem doesn't like herself, she becomes suspicious of anyone that could love her for who she is and then rebuffs the nice guy and subsequently a chance for someone to really respect and cherish her. If she did respect and accept herself, she wouldn't feel the need to chase after the bad boy and put herself in the continual roller coaster ride of highs and lows and the elusive promise of happiness that never quite arrives. She almost always feels the need to try to change the bad boy and justify his infidelities, alcohol or drug habit, and the way he treats people. Hey, he takes no crap from people! Isn't that attractive? No, not really. Not to mature people who have grown up.

He does all these things to justify to the woman he is with that she just doesn't quite measure up yet, so he has to cheat or do something else to send the message she needs to be better. Girls and women with low self-esteem fall for this all the time. Trust me; I tell women to fall for a nice guy because he won't be nice forever. He just doesn't know how to court and bring that level of challenge that a girl wants right off the bat. However, over time, the nice guy facade will wear away and he'll become like every other human being with wants and needs. He then becomes the challenge she wants and at least she knows that in the end, he will treat her with respect and still accept her, faults and all.

To further explain, let me give you an example of female behavior. Interestingly enough, a study was done and it found that women are happier when their husband does more housework. The problem is that during this same time frame, they also found that a wife is less sexually attracted to her husband. In fact, these same studies also show that the husband gets less sex in these cases when he does more work around the house. Wow. No wonder women have so many relationship problems. So it goes back to my Prince Charming Fantasy Theory. Most women want to have sex with an illusion or someone who does things that appear manly and men doing housework is not a turn on for them. So let me say this: it takes real resolve for a woman to find the right partner, to not to settle for something less, and to reward that person for helping them out. When a woman has self-esteem, a man who helps out around the house would or should be seen as someone secure in his masculinity, even if he is doing the dishes. However, to a woman with lower self-esteem and living in a fantasyland, they seem to need to imagine someone above the mundane chores of life to be turned on, which is a big mistake. There is nothing wrong with fantasy in life and in the bedroom, but it should include a partner that is not on the outside looking in. If that happens, you are doing it wrong.

To put it altogether, it is very important for a daughter to seek the right person to share her dreams and help make her life a success. This is accomplished by using real resolve to put life's needs versus wants in perspective to find the right person to be truly happy. Fortunately, it can all begin when a dad points out to his daughter what qualities to admire in another person and which ones are suspect. Yes, dads know the male species well and because of that, his daughter has a chance at a wonderful life.

Let's move on and talk about general resolve and a true story of a man named Tim. He was in a car accident so severe that he was in a coma for two weeks. He also had severe head and spinal cord injuries, nearly had his leg severed, and was paralyzed. Through three years of rehabilitation, he moved from his wheelchair to a walker and eventually to a cane. However, the story doesn't end there. He later switched professions and became a registered nurse to help those similar to him in a neurotrauma unit and even earned a police certification to further help even more people. This is the type of resolve we all should have in life—to not give up no matter what happens to us. So ask yourself: do you have this type of resolve? Are you using this type of resolve? Both answers should be yes if you want to overcome your obstacles and fulfill your dreams.

You may also recall the story of New York Yankee great, Lou Gehrig being stuck down by a horrible illness called amyotrophic lateral sclerosis (ALS), a neurodegenerative disease that causes rapid weakness because of muscle atrophy. Gehrig was so famous that when he was struck by the disease, people around the world simply called it, "Lou Gehrig's Disease." Ironically, Gehrig was called "The Iron Horse" for playing in 2,130 consecutive games. During that streak, Gehrig suffered several bone fractures, including some that he was unaware of. In two different games, he was knocked unconscious but stayed in that game and played in the next one. One day, he was hit by severe back pain so the manager let him lead off the game. He promptly singled before he was replaced. Another time, he was thrown out early in a game by an umpire, but he had already batted, and of course, having the flu was never a problem.

If Lou could walk, he was playing. He simply had the resolve to keep playing for his fans, teammates, parents, and his wife through that streak. But most importantly, he had the inner resolve to do it for himself. In fact, little did he know, he was fighting a futile battle but refused to quit. In 1937, he had noticed the start of physical change. Despite his statistics being slightly down, he fought on. Finally in Detroit in 1938, he went to the manager and took himself out so he wouldn't hurt the team. It was at this point that not only had he lost all his power, he could hardly hold the bat. He had given it everything he had. To those around Gehrig, they remembered him not for a disease, but for the resolve he showed day in and day out. The Yankees eventually gave him a special day to honor him and that occurred at Yankee Stadium on July 4th, 1939, where Gehrig gave one of the most famous speeches in history. In that speech, he gave thanks to thousands of baseball fans for the support, kindness, and encouragement he had received. He was dying, and yet called himself, "the luckiest man on the face of the earth." This story has been well told. But what you may not remember is that he was given a poem as a gift that was originally written by John Greenleaf Whittier called "Don't Quit." It's a long poem best read in its entirety, but let me share just a few key lines:

> When things go wrong as they sometimes will,
> When the road you're trudging seems all up hill,
> When funds are low and debts are high,
> And you want to smile, but you have to sigh,
> When care is pressing you down a bit,
> Rest if you must, but don't you quit.
> So stick to the fight when you are hardest hit,
> It's when things seem worst that you mustn't quit.

Here's the point: if you live long enough, you are going to run into obstacles where you want to quit. You have to continue on and persevere even when the odds are stacked against you. Also, if you are going to make the most of life, it's not just enough to keep going, but to be better than the day before. Here's what the great UCLA basketball coach, John Wooden said. I keep this posted on my wall at home:

> Remember this your lifetime through:
> Tomorrow there will be more to do.
> And failure waits for those who stay,
> With some success made yesterday.
> Tomorrow you must try once more,
> And even harder than before.

Let me also tell you a side story about that Wooden quote and resolve. I had written to the Wooden family to ask permission to use it because I thought it was a great quote that would help many people. However, their initial offer was a little high and based on my overall expenses, I could not afford it and told them so. A counter offer came back that was still too high in my estimation. So I thanked the Wooden family and said it was okay because I had written another poem myself and I explained my situation in more detail. In fairness to them, it was not until they fully understood my budget and the actual project that I received an email back that said to, "Consider this e-mail as permission to use the quote." This was a kind gesture that restored by faith in humanity. Now, don't get me wrong: had I used that quote for another project where it was prominently displayed, it would have been worth every penny they were asking. In this case, good communication and resolve won out. I like to think that somewhere, John Wooden himself would be looking down and smiling at my perseverance and resolve to make this world a better place.

Now you may be thinking, did you really write another poem that quickly? Yes I did. You see, an important part of life and what you will be remembered for is your integrity and honesty. That is what you take to the grave with you as people remember you. So here is that poem I scratched out in front of the television between e-mails:

> Yesterday is over, there's nothing more to do.
> The choice made today, however, will always carry you.
> So forget about the awards, success, and laurels—and living in the past.
> They bring you down with complacency, and it can happen pretty fast.
> Yes, tomorrow is the real day to try harder than before,
> To exceed the success of yesterday, to open every door.
> So push yourself to newer heights and rise above the rest,
> And give each day everything you've got to be your very best.

Regardless of the poem or any other form of motivation you may relate to, the point is clear: not only must you continue on and persist in life, you also have to try to continue to achieve and be more than you were yesterday. This is the key to those who really want and do succeed and those who don't reach their goals. Some people achieve some level of success and rest on their laurels while some are afraid to try at all. However in life, one success builds upon another. This is what every dad needs to get his daughter to understand.

Of course, part of resolve is being dedicated to life 100 percent, not 99 percent. I was once handed a paper that was entitled, "If 99.9 Percent is Good Enough." As I glanced at the sheet, there were some interesting claims. I am not sure how true they are, but they make a point. It states that if 99.9 percent effort is good enough, then:

- 12 newborns will be given to the wrong parents daily.
- 315 entries in Webster's dictionary will be misspelled.
- Two planes landing at Chicago's O'Hare airport will be unsafe every day.
- Over 103,260 tax returns will be processed incorrectly.
- 291 pacemaker operations will be performed incorrectly.

Several other things were also listed, but the point is clear again: give all you can and then go and give a little more. When you make it a habit to go the extra mile in your resolve, you can accomplish great things. Of course perspective should also be kept in mind. For instance, if the police solved 99.9 percent of their cases, that would be seen as very successful. Or if a chef cooked a meal where 99.9 percent of the food made it on the plate, then that also would be successful to most people. The key is to just do more than you promised and go the extra mile and things will turn out better in the long run. It's the attention to detail and getting things done that will open doors for any daughter.

Another issue is that sometimes we don't have a lot of help in our own struggle and it can get frustrating. If this is true for you, consider this guy named Jesus. He walked the earth like you and I, but Jesus changed the world for eternity despite many obstacles. He was born in a stable, had no office, and not much money. Furthermore, it appears He never traveled more than 200 miles from his house. He had no degree or credentials, was denied by His friends, and mocked and spat upon during his trial. He was crucified like a criminal with thieves, lost His clothes in a dice game, and was buried in a borrowed tomb. In between these events, however, He simply tried to love people. Because of this persistence and resolve in doing so in the face of adversity, He became the greatest man to ever walk the earth. Jesus became a good example of the internal perseverance and gritty resolve that we all need and that a daughter needs to learn from both her earthly father and hopefully, if so inclined, her heavenly father. Here are some resolve rules you can follow:

- Persistence, dedication, and determination decide your future.
- Talent, genius, and education mean nothing unless you use them.
- Begin each day with a forgiving spirit. Start by forgiving yourself.
- Be accountable for your life and don't blame others. Otherwise, you remain stuck.
- Take action toward your goals every day.
- Seek advice from mentors, books, tapes, and other resources.
- Turn your knowledge into wisdom. Knowledge helps us to understand that a tomato is a fruit. Wisdom helps us understand you don't put a tomato in a fruit salad.
- Choose friends wisely who bring out the best in you and hold you to a higher standard.
- Let criticism slide off your back.
- Learn to make great decisions and change your mind slowly.
- Choose to be happy.
- Learn from your past. It will help guide your future.
- Take educated risks. This is how successful people succeed.
- Improve yourself daily, even if the change is small. Over time, it looms large.
- Remember John Wooden: "So tomorrow try once more, and even harder than before."

To pull it all together, how can a dad further help with resolve and what are some other things a daughter must remember? I believe it's important that a dad never rain on his daughter's dreams, while also passing along the notion that realistic expectations are okay and can produce a happy life. By keeping these objectives in mind, he can help guide her life and show her that despite glamour magazines, movies, and television, a daughter doesn't need to be a rock and roll diva for life to be rewarding. However, if she wants to pursue these dreams, even seemingly unrealistic dreams, a dad needs to stand by her.

Remember this: some of the most successful people in life were discouraged or told they couldn't so something. Instead of agreeing with that prognosis, they listened to their inner voice, followed their own path, and succeeded. Regardless of any success achieved, a dad must be there with his arm around his daughter, supporting her all the way and encouraging her to keep going when the bumps in the road come. By contrast, as I mentioned earlier, she will be monitoring her dad to see how he bounces back from adversity himself and will see the kind of inner strength he has as well. In fact, setting an example is the strongest way to get others to follow your lead. If a dad can show and help a daughter to find both kindness and persistence inside of herself and strength in her beliefs and goals, it will keep her on the right path to success in all facets of her life. A daughter should also remember this: always listen with an open heart if a dad feels some pursuits are unrealistic and that it's time to move on. While that doesn't mean you will always follow that advice or that it is always correct, opening your ears and relying on dad's common sense and logic can make life a lot easier at times. Finally, when you get stuck in life and need some hope, refer to these quotes that I use to keep myself going:

- "For I know the plans I have for you," declares the Lord. "Plans to prosper you and not harm you." (Jeremiah 29:11)
- "Seek first the Kingdom of God, and everything will be added unto you." (Matthew 6:33)
- "There are two types of pain you will go through in life: the pain of discipline and the pain of regret." (Jim Rohn)
- "Therefore I tell you, whatever you ask for in prayer, believe that you have received it and it will be yours." (Mark 11:24)
- "If God is for me, who can be against me." (Romans 8:31)

The Resolve Secret Summary: The key to resolve is the ability to overcome adversity and bumps in the road to get things done. It's the ability to look at the bigger purpose and passions in life to jump over the temporary setbacks. It's the ability to stay focused on your goals until you achieve them despite times when things are falling apart all around you. Resolve also means not resting on your accomplishments, giving life a true 100 percent effort, and being responsible for your own happiness. Finally, dads can be great examples of resolve and in the end, both fathers and daughters can and should lift each other up through life when times get tough by exhibiting true resolve.

CHAPTER FOURTEEN

# THE SUPPORT SECRET

*"Keep away from people who try to belittle your ambitions. Small people always do that, but the really great will make you feel that you, too, can become great."*
–Mark Twain

The truth is this: everyone needs some type of support in this world and no one really walks the path in life alone, though they may try. We depend on others to help keep us going so we can succeed in life. Although we, alone, are responsible for our happiness and the choices and decisions we make that often determine the success or failure we have in life, these choices often come from the environmental influence and guidance of others through life experience. This is why we need to find trusted sources of people to support us on our journey. As you may well know, this is not always easy. We may respect one person's opinion and perhaps ignore another person based on our interaction, the trust level with that person, and our own gut feeling. Regardless of our method, criteria, or reasons for choosing the people we lean on, it is vitally important to find people to support us in life so we can be all that we are meant to be.

Success-related support itself comes in many forms, including physical, financial, spiritual, and emotional support. As you can expect, all these various forms of support are important to being the person we want to be as we head to self-actualization, which again, is reaching one's full potential. Next, we should understand that a dad needs to give this kind of help to his daughter. There might be differing levels to it and on occasion, it should be reciprocated to show respect and that she is capable of giving the same to her children someday. For instance, it may be obvious that a daughter likely would not support a dad financially nor should she be expected to as she is growing up. But she can be there emotionally to help him with a hug or kind words. However, what if he was an old man and short of resources? Then perhaps she should help him out financially. What if a dad helps his daughter by changing her diaper, helping her ride a bike or drive a car, or puts bandages on when she hurts herself? Then that can or should be reciprocated as he grows older by physically taking care of him or making sure others are looking after him.

It's the same with an emotional and spiritual life as well. You can laugh together, cry together, hug each other, kiss each other and generally give the other person hope to go on. This is what family and support is all about. When this happens and people work together, life becomes a satisfying two-way street where people rely on and support each other. Unfortunately, some people get caught up in the blame game, trying to figure out how much to reciprocate by figuring out what the other person has done to help them. However, the real reason to help is because you can without wondering what you will get back. When you do that, you will feel good about yourself by showing the essence of true support. Therefore, support should be given regardless of reciprocation. Simply put, life is often a series of highs and lows for all people. A dad and a daughter can and should support each other and other people, not only those that are close to them or that they care about, but the disadvantaged and downtrodden if possible. In fact, true happiness often comes when people take it one step further and care and support people they hardly know with the full realization they will not get back anything in return. In the ultimate game of life, people need people and anyone who doesn't think so is likely a fool.

While I have touched on various types of support, for the purposes of this chapter, I want to discuss emotional support; a specific support which must be given unconditionally, regardless of whether a daughter is perceived as an unbelievable success or if she is someone who has failed in her own eyes. However, let's say this first: in a father's eyes, she should never be considered a failure no matter what she does. This is especially important in a dad and daughter relationship where love and support should be unconditional or as I like to say, with no strings attached.

For instance, life often presents circumstances that can be like riding a bike for the first time. Think back to when you were a child and attempting to ride a two-wheel bike for the first time and the training wheels were removed. Sure, some kids were off and flying like it was second nature, but most of us fell down a few times, bruised a knee, and scraped a shin. Now imagine your dad is overseeing this life milestone. How he reacts to you falling and the other bumps life presents can determine the emotional security blanket we need to get up and try again. Though similar to resolve, this is different. In resolve, we make the decision to fight through a situation and try again. With support from others, it gives us confidence to succeed and energizes our resolve.

Now imagine a scenario where a daughter falls off her bike and her dad says, "Darn it, I knew we were doing this too soon. Why are we even doing this? You're just going to beat yourself up!" Now imagine the same scenario, but this time, her dad says, "Well honey, I fell a few times as well. You just have to pick yourself up and try again until you can ride that bike." Whose dad would you want? Whose dad do you think would have the more successful daughter if approached like this in a continual manner in life? The first dad does nothing but put pressure on his daughter. The second dad gives her hope and communicates that there are bumps along the way but she can reach her goal if she keeps trying. Hopefully you chose the second dad in that scenario and realize the importance of encouraging words and support and the effect they make on another person, especially if repeated over time.

Riding a bike may seem like a minor milestone in life. However, imagine the major milestones or bumps in the road that will definitely come her way—things like family relationship issues, sex issues, drugs, heartbreak over any issue, illness or disease, work issues, marriage, divorce, death of a family member, or any number of other things. Now imagine the success of overcoming these issues if a very supportive father is in place to support his daughter in a positive way. We can also imagine the contrast that a non-supportive father would bring and how it would subsequently lend itself to the dysfunctional way a daughter may approach these same issues and therefore pick poor resolutions to her problems. Without the ability of a father to guide her in a positive way, a daughter will tend to not only make poor decisions, but impulsive ones. Usually these are the choices that don't benefit her. In fact, not only are these decisions not well thought out, they may be chosen just to keep the peace with others or are even consciously or unconsciously as a form of self-sabotage. With the emotional support of a father who will support and guide her in a positive way, a better decision can be made and good decisions over time will dramatically improve her life.

For a daughter, emotional support first begins and is felt deeply at the gut level. While most people have some intuitive sense, the female gender in particular is tuned into what is commonly referred to as "women's intuition." This ability of heightened intuition, whether in a young girl or an older woman, helps them sense and feel in their core if they are really being emotionally supported regardless of the circumstances, her superficial looks, or her accomplishments. Based on research, this intuitive skill is actually honing the ability to read facial expressions, sharing their emotions more to gather feedback, and spending more time observing other people. It seems to be a different way of paying attention to other people than the average male, although men have strong if not different intuition gathered in other ways. Regardless, a dad can be important in honing a daughter's intuition about the world and can be providing an emotional safety net or parachute that can help with a safer and softer landing when she is confronted with the major issues in life. When this happens and she senses that dad cares and will listen to her, it gives her the feeling and, dare I say, "intuition," that someone is on her side when life gets rough.

Another important aspect of support for a dad to consider and reinforce is the notion that nobody is perfect. Because of that, it should be obvious that he always needs to give his daughter the room to be imperfect as well.

Sometimes for a parent, it's not that easy. Why? It's because we want our children to be successful at everything they do. Although every dad wants his daughter to be the best she can be, when she or anyone else is riding under the pressure of induced perfectionism, it does not cause things to get done and be better. Rather, it can paralyze a person into inaction when facing that kind of additional scrutiny. I think, as individuals, we can and should want to strive to be perfect and be the best person we can be. However, as I touched on earlier, a father that expects his daughter to be perfect to the point of perfectionism ends up with a daughter who is not only unhappy, but rigid in both her experience and existence in life. We must remember that most human beings that learn from their mistakes go on to create some of their biggest triumphs and successes out of these errors. Someone like Thomas Edison, who created his best inventions after many failures, might tell you the same thing. So remember, being afraid of making mistakes is not only no way to live, it actually deters and prevents real progress.

Let's hear Joanie's story—a daughter who went to work for her father:

> My dad was a pay-attention-to-detail kind of guy; he expected a lot of others and himself. He always arrived early, plans were set, and everything was like clockwork. Now all these things about my dad can be great things to be, but on a continuous strict schedule, I felt like I was losing my autonomy and ability to be spontaneous. After some time, resentment formed as I tried to keep up with the pace. At some point, I realized I was different. I had a different temperament and personality. I eventually explained that to my dad and over time, I was able to show him I could be effective doing things my way. I still embraced punctuality and planning, but also allowed time for spontaneity and creativity to come into my life. Luckily, my dad listened, supported my new way of doing things, and was still there for me when I needed advice. He did not reject me or tell me to figure it out on my own because I didn't totally embrace the way he did things. This emotional support and acceptance from my dad was

important and the unexpected benefit was that he also changed in a positive way as well. He became a little less rigid—not just with me, but others as well.

In the end, Joanie wanted support from her dad, but she also wanted to breathe and be her own person and she made that happen.

I also believe a dad should encourage his daughter's dreams, not put a damper on them. In fact, everyone needs to dream and follow their aspirations and endeavors. Without a dream or something to hope for, what value would life have? It is these dreams and aspirations that make people want to save the world, help people, achieve peace, find love, make others happy, become successful, and reach the pinnacle of self-awareness and self-actualization. These things are all great, but a dad is also important in shaping a daughter's dreams and guiding her to choices that are more realistic over time. For example, you wouldn't expect a 300-pound man to be a horse jockey. Nor would you expect a daughter to be an opera singer if she can't carry a tune. Of course, therein lies the secret to support: if a daughter's dreams to be a movie star or glamorous model don't pan out and come to fruition, dad needs to be there to pick up the pieces with non-judgmental support and guidance. It is this continuous emotional support from a father that keeps his daughter emotionally grounded and secure through life, builds her confidence, and adds value to her life. When she has this type of support as part of her life experience, it allows her to treat others with the same values, support, and equality of autonomy. In other words, if she is emotionally supported, she can reach out and support others.

Another important reason for being supportive is that it builds confidence and self-esteem in a daughter. The reason for this is that when a daughter has good self-esteem, she is better able to handle the emotional and psychological storms that life will throw at her. After all, there is always someone who will try to rain on the parade. In prep school, it might be the bully or the one that leaves a broken heart. As we get older, it might be a boss, spouse, or an unfaithful friend. Unfortunately, it seems like when someone tries to rise in life, we can always count on someone who wants to bring them down—a sad indictment indeed.

When this happens, trust then becomes an issue. So for real intimate and emotional support through our life's journey, we can and do often turn to our parents and siblings initially. If we are lucky, later on, we may have a similar connection with a significant other. However, because spousal relationships tend to not work out in this day and age, many people rely on a parent's guidance for a different perspective well into adulthood. Regardless, for a daughter from the very beginning, the consistently best connection is her dad if she wants to reach the pinnacle of success and happiness according to research. This is because she may see him as a protector her entire life, as someone who is bigger, stronger, and with an opinion that is different than everyone else's and solely centered on helping her with fairness and objectivity to help give her more insight. Dad also provides an opposite gender view which provides a different understanding about the world. This leads to even more sustained confidence and success, much like a mother and son who have a similar and strong connection themselves. This is because males tend to be logical thinkers and females tend to be emotional thinkers. When these ways of thinking are combined and understood, they give a person more reasoning ability. Therefore, a father gives the tools of awareness to his daughter to choose success on a consistent basis and to soften the blows in life. For instance, a dad can communicate and explain in detail to his daughter that other kids and even adults can be cruel and don't always have her best interests in heart. Hearing this from a male and mentoring perspective appears to register differently for a daughter and becomes a more innate part of her core. It is this preemptive planning and explaining that prepares her mentally and helps her let insults and injury slide off her back. Simply put, a daughter who has awareness and good self-esteem doesn't feel inferior to others, has a harder time being bullied, and most importantly, feels supported enough to keep going and succeed. The research is clear: much of this potential confidence and success is connected to her dad.

This should go without saying, but a dad should be an example to his daughter and stay away from the name-calling or snide comments that may be directed toward others that come into her life or that may even be directed toward his own daughter. Let's be honest: at times, this is hard to do when a father perceives someone is not treating his daughter the way he would like (or the way he would treat her) or when he becomes frustrated with her over the choices she has made. Let's be clear: this is not to say he shouldn't be assertive and make his point known to his daughter and other people in her life, because that is an imperative and important part of the learning experience for her. However, it need not be aggressive and diverge to the point where good communication is hopeless because people can't keep their cool or because they go off topic. When this happens, the focus or lesson of the subject is lost, often on deaf ears. So when those times come around that dad can be an example in taking the high road in getting his point across properly, it means his credibility increases in the eyes of his daughter and she has no excuse in making similar negative comments to others. It also means that when a dad uses assertive and appropriate communication with other people, he provides the model of how she should also communicate. In that sense, a dad further supports his daughter by having her understand what proper support communication look like and what it shouldn't look like. In other words, learning and knowing how to express your feelings and inner being is an important aspect of support that is communicated at first from a father to a daughter, to others, and then back from a daughter to her father. We must remember, however, that there is a fine line between a dad giving unconditional support in her choices (with the ability to be autonomous in her reactions) and how she treats others. For instance, a dad should want a daughter to express who she is from the core of her being, but in an appropriate way that effectively uses her communication skills with those she comes into contact with so she can become more successful, as opposed to sabotaging herself and her future with ill-timed words and actions. Therefore, it can be said that effectively supporting others often reciprocally increases a person's own value, support, and success in life, and so it is with a daughter.

There will also be challenges to support and it is not always easy, as I touched on before. This can happen when a daughter makes the same mistakes over and over and doesn't learn from them, because she is rebellious, or in a case like divorce, where communication may be difficult because of the dynamics of a blended relationship or because of time apart from each other. In essence, the key for a dad in emotionally supporting his daughter is just to be there to listen to her, to give a hug and shoulder to cry on, and to help her pick up the pieces. Isn't that what we all need, as human beings?

Understandably, it is difficult for a dad to keep his patience during these roller coaster rides and unpredictable times that a daughter goes through to the point it may even test his own resolve and inner strength. But in the end, and as I have written before, it is vital that a dad be there for his daughter. If he cannot be there physically, it's important she feel the presence and guidance of his values and spirit of doing the right thing. Conversely, a daughter should support her father in a reciprocal bond that enhances closeness, communication, and respect. This level of support becomes especially important even if a dad is a man of few words and does most of the listening while his daughter does most of the talking. In the end, regardless of a dad's verbal skills, sometimes lending an ear and a hug may be all we need as people to make a difference in each other's lives. We must support each other.

**The Support Secret Summary: Everyone needs support in this journey called life. Emotional support is among the most important types of support for a daughter. How a dad reacts to the bumps in his own life and subsequently his daughter's life can have a significant impact on how she approaches her own journey and how successful she'll eventually be. Support is especially important when major trials and tribulations come her way. Therefore, positive emotional support from a father given on a consistent basis can make all the difference in the world to his daughter.**

CHAPTER FIFTEEN

# THE SPIRITUAL LIFE SECRET

*"I want to know God's thoughts. The rest are details."*
–Albert Einstein

What is the ultimate purpose of your life? What higher good does your life represent? Is simply existing and leading a life of quiet desperation, as Thoreau ascertained, enough for each of us? Would doing whatever you wanted in life, followed by a permanent death, be satisfying to your higher intellectual and emotional reasoning? By contrast, is there a higher calling and deeper meaning to each of our lives that would build a better society and fulfill God's plan? To me personally, there is nothing more important than the life-giving force of a spiritual life. A spiritual life or spiritual guidance is something that a dad can pass on to his daughter.

Looking back on my own life, an evolving and growing spiritual path has always been a part of a deeper need within me and something I've always yearned for more than anything else. I believe this is vital to every person. Why? Take a moment to imagine the happiest person in the world. Even this person, if he or she is considered normal by today's society, will alternate between varying degrees of happiness and sadness, elation and suffering, euphoria and pain, and finally, joy and despair. Now think of those folks that are really suffering. Some of these people are continually stuck with constant and chronic physical, emotional, and psychological pain. Despite Abraham Lincoln saying that most people are as happy as they make up their minds to be, some seem to have no choice but to suffer, seemingly with no hope. Therefore, it makes sense that a spiritual life seems imperative to keep moving on. Also, no matter what any person achieves or acquires, or any proclamation that they live their life to the fullest measure, I believe they can never be truly happy or fulfilled unless they are filled with the life-giving force of a spirit that engulfs them with a cause greater than themselves and their fellow man. This is because no matter what our acquisition and material desires are, even if we are lucky enough to acquire or possess them, they eventually leave us empty and wanting for more things to fill the emptiness within us. In fact, over my lifetime, I have watched a few people give up considerable wealth and most of their possessions to live the simple life. At first, I thought this was a little nutty. What makes some people give up millions of dollars to live in a small log cabin or a miniature trailer? What makes some people give up Wall Street and the rat race to live in nature, eat edible flowers, and gather water from a stream? It is this intense desire to live in peace, tranquility, nature, and to find out who they really are while exploring their spiritual self. Let me add this: these people seem happier when they make these changes and report that they are happier. This may not be the ideal path for everyone, but it describes the quest to really get in touch with ourselves that most of us have.

Some will say there is no hope for those on earth. I am here to say that there is hope and it is within our spirit. Material goods and prestigious awards cannot take the sorrow away when you are in pain. The only way to achieve this ultimate goal of true happiness and satisfaction is to try to actively nurture our life-giving spirit throughout our lives. Perhaps these lives of quiet desperation that people lead are actually folks who are running from God hoping that some temporary satisfaction here and there will get them to the end of their lives. I am here to tell you that is no way to live and it simply doesn't work because our conscious guides us and beats us up when we take the lower road instead of the higher road and become stuck. That's why getting even with someone is never a good idea; you will eventually pay for it. I won't mention their names, but I can think of two high-profile, "crime of the century" criminal cases where the defendant was found not guilty but wound up back in the headlines because they couldn't stay out of trouble despite the incredible second chance they were given. It seemed like their self-conscious was almost sabotaging them.

Some may disagree with this as well, but I feel this life is a preparation for the next life. Doesn't it stand to reason that there has to be something better out there than this life can offer? Also, when pressed, no one can seem to come up with a better answer or solution to guide our future. I, for one, am not somebody that says when you die, your life is over and there is nothing you can do about it. That sounds so depressing! Also, what about this life on earth? You need a spirit force to make it through this life on earth before we can even talk about an afterlife. That's why I believe in a life-giving spiritual force that is within me, guiding me to a better tomorrow and a brighter future that will last forever.

Yes, this is where a spiritual life comes in. Believing in a higher power satisfies our soul and senses and gives us hope. Without hope and dreams, we become miserable and live like a rowboat being tossed by an angry ocean and often are controlled by the events in our life. Perhaps that's why it's both amazing and almost expected now to see the amount of people turning back to a spiritual life after finding that material possessions like cars, houses, pools, country clubs, and money offered no real or long-lasting happiness. These things can make life easier but do not meet the deep-seeded emotional needs every human being longs for deep inside their soul. In fact, this may also explain why one study found that 96 percent of people believe in God, nine out of ten identify with a religious denomination, and 57 percent attend religious services regularly. People simply want more, not only in this life, but perhaps in another life after this one comes to an end. In addition, the communication barriers between human beings have grown which has helped turn more people to a higher power. Neighbors now do their own thing, families are spread across the country, the work place has become a more politically correct place where we can't discuss our inner or spiritual thoughts, and when people do come around, it seems like some of that time is buried in a cell phone.

Most of us dream of and are hungry for being nurtured, cared about, and really loved. So when other people let us down and these basic human needs are not met, there may be two paths that appear before us that we can take. Most will take the broader and more destructive path filled with vices like drugs, alcohol, revenge bitterness, and other unsuccessful coping mechanisms. The other choice that fewer, but seemingly more enlightened people take is the narrower, less traveled path. This path eventually leads to turning to a spiritual side and higher power that understands us and that can potentially create the deep satisfaction, fulfillment, and happiness we all crave.

Not surprisingly, however, it's not always the challenging and enlightening path that wins out. Why? This is because it takes discipline to stay the course to reach our ultimate destination and humans like to reward themselves with things that reward immediate gratification regardless of the consequences. In fact, this broad path to destruction keeps them distracted with various vices and veers them off course with immediate and temporary pleasures that people use to create what I would call a self-induced coma. Unfortunately, this means walking through life without a true higher purpose—one that keeps them from living life in a straightforward way. In fact, it can keep them from ever finding the narrow and right path few have the courage to travel. Our society simply wants to medicate ourselves with things we know won't help us instead of strengthening the spiritual life inside and serving a higher power like God.

For this chapter, I am going to refer to my higher power as God or Jesus, without apology. Everyone has to choose what they feel works for them and I know what works for me. It might also be worth noting that in my opinion, there is a difference in saying you believe in God or a higher power and truly following and obeying God or what you believe. As God clearly states, "If you believe in me, then you obey me." A spiritual life has reaped benefits for both dads and their daughters over time and allowed them to push on with life.

Research shows that when it comes to believing in and obeying a higher power, there is strong evidence that it is beneficial to a daughter and everyone else. For instance, studies show the stronger believe in a higher power like God or Jesus, the stronger correlation in the prevention of deviant behaviors like premarital sex and taking recreational drugs. If this is just from simple belief, what would happen if we also teach a daughter to pray, pray with her, take her to church (whatever your conception of church is), talk to her about spiritual things, or have her participate in various spiritual or religious activities or services? What usually happens is it further strengthens her life path, lessens stress, prevents deviant behaviors, gives her peace, may ultimately save her life, and as a bonus, gets her to heaven if you believe in an afterlife. Of course, a dad must remember that this can't be coerced and manipulated, but must be done with sincerity. Who wouldn't want these benefits? It also helps if a dad models the same beliefs and behaviors in his search of a higher power or God because being a role model in this area for what he wants to convey is the ultimate teaching tool.

The benefits don't stop there. Those who pursue a spiritual life tend to have more contact with good and positive friends, feel happier, have more self-esteem, have a better attitude, and get better grades. They also tend to be better adjusted both mentally and emotionally. Aren't these the qualities and character traits you want in your daughter?

If you are a dad or daughter with a strong spiritual side, I applaud you. For those who have wanted a spiritual life but struggled, who have been hurt by a church, or who have thought a spiritual life wasn't or isn't important or necessary, it might benefit you and is worth looking into. To help that path, I have created some guidelines and suggestions and borrowed some bible verses that may help. In fact, if you have struggled with believing and obeying God or you feel He hasn't been there for you, read on; there is hope.

## HOW TO GET CLOSER TO GOD

- Do you really believe? Realize that only God could make a pumping station like your heart, a filtering system like your kidneys, a computer like your brain, a support structure like the arch of your foot, and your own individual fingerprints out of billions of people.

- Examine and resolve the inner motivation of your life. A spiritual life will shift your focus from fear, guilt, control, anger, material possessions, the approval of others, and the unrealistic expectations you have for yourself. Instead, find the purpose within that gives life meaning. Often, this means giving to others and focusing on your spiritual self and your higher power/God.
- Simplify your life. Focus on God and your relationship with Jesus. Simplify your focus and motivation. This helps you do the things that get you ready for heaven and keeps you from being overwhelmed by the minutiae of life.
- Remember that your life is not an accident, you have a destiny, and that destiny is God's purpose, not your own. Once you learn that, life is easier. If you rebel against God, life gets harder.
- Life on earth is short when compared to eternity. Think of it this way: it's like a drop of water in the ocean. It's like a sand of grain on a beach. Do you want to spend billions of years in heaven or hell? How is that for motivation? Guess what; it's your choice.
- Consider this: if you wonder if there is a heaven or a God and you are wrong, no harm, no foul. You have bettered humanity with kindness. However, if you live like there is no afterlife and you are wrong—game over.
- Consider life like a video game. We are basically judged by God for what we do here on earth. When you follow God, you get bonus points and rewards stored in heaven. When you don't do what you are supposed to do, points are taken away. Have a goal of entering heaven with maximum points and rewards that last forever.
- God said, "He that is not with Me is against Me" (Matthew 12:30). Who wants to be against God? Not me.
- You are not smarter than God. Let him be in control. Don't say you trust in God and do your own thing. Your heart already knows what God wants.
- Make a mission statement of what you'll accept in your life and

what you won't. You'll soon notice that if you are improving your spiritual life, both lists become obvious over time.
- Produce good fruit in your life: love, joy, peace, patience, kindness, goodness, faithfulness, gentleness, and self-control (paraphrased from Galatians 5:22–23).
- Push evil desires away; that would be greed, hate, murder, envy, fighting, lying, bitterness, and gossip (see Romans 1:29). I would add lust, slander, adultery, and jealousy as well. Everyone is tempted, but God will not let the burden become unbearable.
- During periods of temptation, call on God and stay out of situations or areas where you tend to give in to weakness. Instead, do something else like praying during these spiritual battles, remembering that salvation is the helmet of God and your sword is the Holy Spirit.
- Develop your spiritual life:
  - God wants you to be happy. Obey Him, thank Him, and believe you already have whatever you have asked for.
  - If God is your reason for living, let love be your guide. When in doubt, love some more.
  - Give glory to God and worship Him to bring Him happiness. Remember, everything we do equals worship.
  - Be straight with God. He knows your thoughts before you do and answers in His own time.
  - In context, God's word makes sense and He does not contradict himself.
  - Stay in the word of God, not secular expectations because it feels logical, right, or is part of the culture.
  - Another reason to stay in the word is that real spiritual growth is a slow process. Over time, both your spirituality and character are revealed, so be patient.
  - Be like Jesus in your walk, remembering His spiritual approach, trials, and tribulations. Think to yourself, "I am not the only one who has a challenging path."
  - Be in constant prayer, especially praying when you get up and when you go to bed.

- Remember and apply the bible verse, "Seek first the Kingdom of God and his righteousness and everything shall be added unto you" (Matthew 6:33). This quote can be a real motivator.
- Abundant life comes from God (Jehovah), Jesus, and the Holy Spirit. Pray in their names.
- Remember your relationship with Jesus/God is a personal one and not just an association with a religious affiliation.
- Be baptized in the Holy Spirit.
- Remember, "The man who isn't a Christian can't understand and can't accept these thoughts from God, which the Holy Spirit teaches us. They sound foolish to him, because only those who have the Holy Spirit within them can understand what the Holy Spirit means" (1 Corinthians 2:14).
- Uplift each other and the body of the church. If you think you may not need the body, then maybe the body needs you.
- Remember you are not perfect, but you are forgiven.
- Be thankful to God for everything.
- Be dedicated and consistent in your walk with God, remembering the adage, "Winners do the right thing all the time."
- Make your spiritual walk a shining light and example to all.
- Improve yourself as a person in general:
  - Accept your faults; don't get too big with pride.
  - "…If anyone is going to boast, let him boast about what the Lord has done and not about himself" (2 Corinthians 10:17–18).
  - Do the best you can with what you have where you are.
  - Journal your thoughts; it will help you understand yourself.
  - Use your gifts, talents, and abilities to serve others. Being a servant is the noblest of professions.
  - Build your honesty, integrity, and character.
  - When we are in rebellion or distress, we want to use "coddle me" prayers and that is understandable. However, as we grow as a person spiritually, we need to have "conform me" or "use me for your purpose" prayers and let God mold us into who we need to be.

- How we should treat and handle other people:
  - Get along with others as much as possible without sacrificing your beliefs.
  - Be in service to others to help them. (Notice I mention to be a servant again.)
  - Tell others about God. By doing so, you serve Him.
  - Love not only those who love you, but also your enemies. Anyone can love those people that love them; that takes little effort. It takes true skill to love those who are hard to love (paraphrased from Luke 6:32).
  - Show empathy and give mercy.
  - Share what you have and help others by giving without expecting anything back.
  - "Don't be selfish, don't live to make a good impression on others. Be humble and courteous, thinking of others as better than yourself" (Philippians 2:3).
  - Don't give to others to bring attention to yourself.
  - Stay away from the three Cs: complaining, criticizing, and condemning.
  - Refuse to spread gossip.
  - Resolve conflicts and issues as quickly as possible.
  - When in doubt, just love them.
  - Ask for forgiveness when you make mistakes.

In conclusion, both life and deciding on a spiritual path may bring up questions you need to ask yourself: why am I on earth? What is my purpose? How can I achieve my purpose? What path do I need to take? How will I serve and contribute to God? How can I win others to God/Jesus/a better spiritual path? These questions remind us this is not an easy path to take and sometimes the storms are all around us. In fact, sometimes we may even question God when turbulence is still hanging around despite our most fervent prayers. When this happens, just remember, sometimes God looks deep into our hearts and calms the storm within us, giving us inner strength to make it bearable to go on. This is what a dad can teach his daughter: she can depend on her inner spirituality and strength to overcome the bumps in the road and the obstacles in life.

Let me add this personal note: I believe Jesus died on a cross for me to give me eternal life. I also understand others will feel differently, but I wanted and desired to serve God and I have come to love that challenge. Again, this is the narrow path and not always earthly rewarded. But don't fret: if you choose this path, you are not alone. There are two bible verses to keep in mind, the first one being, "As I live, every knee will bow to me and every tongue confess to God" (Romans 14:11). God has also said, "Whoever clings to his life shall lose it, and whoever loses his life, shall save it" (Luke 17:33). He knows the trials, tribulations, and dangers of being a Christian or a follower of God. However, He also knows the narrow path of following Him that leads to glory. Finally, it is said we become what we think about most. To change our lives, ponder the word and goodness of God, stay in prayer, and above all, pour out your love to others. In the end, the happiness of a daughter, her dad, and virtually everyone else may be dependent on this thing we call a spiritual life.

**The Spiritual Secret Summary: Spirituality is realizing there is more to life than what is presented here on earth. Pursuing this can put a daughter on the path of finding peace. Material possessions won't make us truly happy and a nurturing relationship with a higher power is important when people let us down. God helps nurture us and understands us so we need to depend on Him. A spiritual life also helps prevent deviant behavior, helps with psychological and emotional health, and helps to improve our relationships. Finally, take the steps to get closer to God because your quality of life is likely dependent on what choices you make.**

CHAPTER SIXTEEN

# IT'S ABOUT THE LOVE SECRET

"Don't worry about the question because love is always the answer"
–Kevin M. Thomas

What is love? Is love really that important in life? How do I get it? How do I give it? These are important questions that I will attempt to define and answer as we go. But let me say this to start: did you know that the bible states that, "love is the only law that you need?" Quite frankly, if you remember nothing else from this book, it is this simple but profound message of love circulating in the world that can change each of us and the destiny of our lives. In fact, love is the very key to life and the most positive and heightened sense of emotion we can have. Most importantly to our discussion here, it is one of the most critical and important concepts for both a daughter and her father to understand.

Think of all your actions and all the laws, rules, and regulations you face in life. Essentially, they all come down to one thing: if you love someone and virtually everyone, eventually everything will be okay. Everything won't always go your way, but if you do the right thing and reach out with love consistently over time, love will usually come back to you in one form or another. Sometimes it will come from other people, sometimes it comes from God, sometimes we don't notice or accept it, and sometimes we want it from someone different than the one who is giving it to us. But love is all around us if we take the time to notice it. More simply put but more staggering to ponder, love is the law of the entire universe regardless of your personal beliefs. But in the view of many, including myself, it comes from the law of God. In fact, if we look closer, God is love and we change our life and the people around us when we give love. This doesn't mean love is always reciprocated or returned and you are not going to get your heart broken or be treated badly. You absolutely will if you live long enough and unfortunately that will happen in a variety of ways. However, in the end, you will come out on top if you approach the rocky road of life with love to give, regardless if it is reciprocated here on earth.

Love can also be one of the most difficult things to define, so I will inject some quotes from others and use my own words to describe it, though words will not do it justice. So what is love? It is an important question and concept because everyone seems to have a different definition for it and most people define it as they perceive it. Therefore, some things that could be unhealthy, risky, or even close to abuse would or could be considered to be love by some people. In addition, a person's level of self-esteem could also determine what they perceive love to be. In fact, this sometimes involves a person choosing someone who is unhealthy over someone who is healthier in the name of "love."

I personally define love between people as an ongoing nurturing experience that is supportive in nature, which helps a person grow in their quest to become all they can be in life, is returned and shared between each person regardless of trials, tribulations, and differences, and ultimately is the strength and bond of that relationship. In addition, true love is not withheld because someone does something that creates disapproval in the other and is always unconditional in nature. Love is not just a matter of the head, but the heart as well. It touches the physical, mental, and spiritual aspects of life and includes all the senses. If someone pulls this nurturing from you because you have made a mistake, then this is not love. If you constantly have to prove yourself for acceptance, this is not love. So, again, therein lies the problem: so many people feel they have to perform or be perfect to get or receive love. This should never be the case for true, unconditional love between two people and should never happen between a father and daughter. Love should always be given freely with no strings attached because that is the very heart of what love is and what it should always be.

This type of relationship of pure acceptance without strings is critical. If a daughter has acceptance and unconditional love to fall back on from her father, her need to try to find love in unhealthy places is greatly diminished. She will have a model of what love really is and what she should accept. For instance, if she feels she is loved by her father, then we can expect she won't be fooled as easily by a future partner who demands tasks or deeds be done to "earn," "achieve," or even keep love. When we love someone, we want to freely do things for them because we love them, not because we want to win their love or are trying to earn it. If conditions are attached to love, this is not really love. With this in mind, a daughter will be able to make good future choices in a mate since she will understand that love is about connecting the head with the heart. She can recognize what love is and what love isn't and therefore be able to view some things in her life as either acceptable or unacceptable. That is, if she is thinking with her head and not just her heart when the butterflies in her belly take over, a condition that often happens in "romantic" love. Unfortunately, some people still have trouble even with all the facts before them and often can't see what everyone else can in this kind of love.

That leads me to another fact I should mention: love tends to defy logic. In fact, love is not only blind in some cases, but sadly, deaf and dumb as well and can be affected by pheromones. This means that our physical desires can override common sense, logic, and reasoning that our head presents us with when it comes to love and what love really is all about. Another issue is realized when true love is given freely but not returned, which can be incredibly painful. In fact, one of the hardest things in life to do is watch the person you love either love someone else when you pour out your heart and soul out to them or they demand things from you to give you "love" back, which can and should convey to us on a deeper level that they really don't love us after all—a painful pill to swallow. So it is important for everyone to keep their ears and eyes open to what real love is and isn't supposed to be and what to look for when it appears. Is it real or a mirage? One way to tell is that true love is given unconditionally.

Next, we also have to understand that constantly trying to earn love makes one fearful with abandonment issues and eventually resentful. A person who is really loved must remember they are loved not just for who they are and the positive qualities they have, but for their quirks, faults, imperfections, and yes, even when they screw up badly. Real love is acceptance of another person as they are, good and bad, over an extended period of time. This shouldn't be confused with the initial infatuation that often shows few faults or flaws if any. In fact, I don't believe you lose real love, in those cases; you may have never had it to being with. That doesn't mean real love is always right or will keep people close in proximity or constantly connected. For instance, every day we see people who love each other but just can't live together, whether that be a family relationship or a romantic connection. However, that doesn't mean real love would lessen in these various tribulations or situations. On the other hand, infatuation can fade quickly and where people can suddenly disappear at the first sign of trouble.

Nurturing love is also important and different than trying to earn love. It simply means explaining or expressing to someone why we love them in a variety of ways. Simply put, it's like giving water to a plant or flower to help it bloom. In regards to a daughter, it almost always helps if a dad points out things to her that make her special, like her compassion, courage, sensitivity to the needs of others, how she treats others, and who she is as a person, among other things. Additionally, I believe other things that should also be emphasized in nurturing a daughter include her character traits and values, inner beauty, and kindness over her physical beauty, although that is important as well, especially if she is insecure about her looks. It is this reinforcement of who she is that will make her blossom as a person.

Not to be redundant, but I cannot emphasize enough that a daughter should feel from a dad that his love is unconditional and is never taken away or reduced because of something she has or hasn't done or said, or because it has to be earned. This doesn't mean he is always happy with her choices or he won't correct or discipline her, but love should always be given freely and unconditionally from father to daughter and from a daughter to her father. This cycle ideally should begin with a father modeling unconditional love in his message and relationships.

I also believe that besides nurturing the traits I mentioned above, a dad should communicate to his daughter that she is special and there is no one else like her. This can really help when those obstacles in the road surely pop up. We know that love from a dad means helping her to hang in there during tough times and rebellion, especially her own teenage rebellion. For instance, almost all children test their parents to varying degrees as they grow up and sometimes dad has the difficult task of doling out discipline. However, at the same time and regardless of her actions, he must not pull away from her emotionally or intellectually and make her understand why discipline is important in helping her grow. He must also keep his own eye on the goal of helping and improving and getting her to be better as a person, instead of giving in to the feeling of wanting to throw in the towel when the frustration comes. True love helps maintain this course and helps to overcome these rough times. This means a dad needs the ability to love persistently, even if she becomes rebellious and nasty and pushes his buttons. That doesn't mean he shouldn't show some anger; even Jesus tipped over a table in the temple when he thought it was being used for illicit gain. However, in the end, it's important to embrace your daughter with strong arms, both literally and figuratively, and simply love her for who she is, not for what she has accomplished or what she looks like on the outside. In the end, it might be said that true love is true acceptance of another human being.

Ever wonder how God would define love? Well he has. One of my favorite bible chapters—1 Corinthians 13:4-7)—describes love beautifully. It states, "Love is very patient and kind, never jealous or envious, never boastful or proud. It is never haughty, or selfish, or rude. It does not demand its own way. It is not irritable or touchy. It does not hold grudges and hardly notices when others do it wrong. It is never glad about injustice, but rejoices whenever truth wins out. If you love someone, you will be loyal to him, no matter what the cost. You always believe in him, always expect the best of him, and always stand your ground in defending him."

Yes, those are very powerful words indeed, but whatever your definition of love is, a dad must make sure it has a nurturing effect on his daughter and conversely, love should be returned. When this happens, love expands, grows from us to other people, then grows in a family, then to a city, then to a state or country. Then it expands to us all as citizens on this big planet, moving like a ripple on a pond connecting us all together to make it a better world. Perhaps all because a dad and his daughter chose to simply grow together in love and by doing so, they ended up loving all those around them.

Finally, I want to conclude this book with a message to my own daughters and to any daughter out there listening: when you fall down, I'll pick you up. When you have dirt on your hands, I will wash them. When you scrape your knee, I will bandage it. When you shed tears, I will kiss them away. When you want to collapse from the struggle, do so in my arms. When you laugh heartily, I am filled with joy. In your brightest of days or loneliest of nights, I will be there for you. I am not perfect. I have made many mistakes and will make more in life. But always know that I am your dad and I will always be there for you. But more importantly, I love you more than you will ever know and I always will.

**The Love Secret Summary: Love is a nurturing experience that touches all emotions and sensibilities. A father's love serves as a model of what love really is and what a daughter should accept in future relationships. A dad's acceptance and unconditional love also helps to prevent deviant and unhealthy love choices a daughter may make. Real love is therefore defined in my opinion as the acceptance of another as they are and should not have to be earned or achieved. So go forward and approach life with love and give love without expecting anything in return. For in the end, giving love really means getting love and love is all you need.**

# REFERENCES

Amato, Hetherington, & Clingempeel. (1992). *Lifespan development* (4th ed.). Boston, MA: Pearson Education.

Boyd, D., & Bee, H. (2006). *Lifespan development* (4th ed.). Boston, MA: Pearson Education.

Cairney, J., & Boyle, M. (2003). Stress, social support, and depression in single and married mothers. *Social Psychiatry and Psychiatric Epidemiology, 38*, 442–449.

Clemens, M. (1997). *Parade.* Hetherington, E., & Martin, B., Family Interaction, *Psychopathological Disorders of Childhood.* New York, NY: John Wiley & Sons.

Coley, R. (1998). Children's socialization experiences and functioning in single-mother households: The importance of fathers and other men. *Child Development, 69*, 219–230.

Davison, K., & Birch, L. (2001). Child and parent characteristics as predictors of change in girls' body mass index. *International Journal of Obesity, 25*(12), 1834–1842. doi:10.1038/sj.ijo.0801835

Duncan, J., Hill, M., & Yeung, W. J. (1996, October). *Fathers' activities and children's attainments.* Paper presented at Father Involvement Conference, Washington D.C.

Esterbrooks, M., & Goldberg, W. (1984). Toddler development in the family: Impact of father involvement and parent characteristics. *Child Development, 55*, 740–752.

Figueroa-Colon, R., Arani, R., Goran, M., & Weinsier, R. (2000). Paternal body fat is longitudinal predictor of changes in body fat in premenarcheal girls. *American Journal of Clinical Nutrition, 71*(3), 829–834.

Forum on Child and Family Statistics (2002). *America's children: Key national indicators of well-being.* Federal Interagency report. Retrieved from http://www.Childstats.gov/pdf/ac2002/front/pdf

Gaudino, J., Jenkins, B., & Rochat, F. (1999). No father's names: A risk factor for infant mortality in the state of Georgia, USA. *Social Science and Medicine, 48*, 253–265.

Goldstein, H. (1982). Father's absence and cognitive development of 12–17-year-olds. *Psychological Reports, 51*, 843–848.

Harknett, K. (2005). *Children's elevated risk of asthma in unmarried families: Underlying structural and behavioral mechanisms.* Working paper. Center for Research and Child Well-Being, Princeton, NJ.

Kelly, J. (2002). *Dads and daughters: How to inspire, understand, and support your daughter.* New York, NY: Broadway Books.

Koestner, R., Franz C., & Weinberger, J. (1990). The family concerns, of empathic concern: A twenty-six year longitudinal study. *Journal of Personality and Social Psychology,58*, 709–717.

Lippman, L. (2004). *Indicators of child, family, and community connections.* Washington DC: Office of the Assistant Secretary for Planning and Evaluation. U.S. Department of Health and Human Services. Retrieved from http://aspe.hhs.gov/hsp/connections-papers04/ papers.pdf

National Center for Education Statistics (1999). *The condition of education.* Washington DC: U.S. Department of Education.

National Fatherhood Initiative. (2004). *Family Structure, Father Closeness, and Delinquency,* (Report from National Fatherhood Initiative). Retrieved from http://www.dadsmove.org/support-files/delinquency 1pg.pdf

National Longitudinal Survey of Youth. (1997). *Study of Obese Children in Father-Absent Homes.* Retrieved from http: http://www.fatherhood.org/statistics-on-father-absence-download

O'Connor, T., Davies, L., Dunn, J., Golding, J., & ALSPAC Study Team. (2000). Differential distribution of children's accidents, injuries and illnesses across family type. *Pediatrics, 106*.

Pedersen, F. (1980). Parent-infant and husband-wife interactions observed at five months. *The Father-Infant Relationship.* New York, NY: Pedersen.

Quinlan, R. J. (2003). Father absence, parental care, and female reproductive development. *Evolution and Human Behavior, 24*, 376–390.

Resnick, M. (2007). Protecting adolescents from harm. *Journal of the American Medical Association, 10*, 823–832.

Schwartz, J. (1995). Socio-demographic and psychosocial factors in childhood as predictors of adult mortality. *American Journal of Public Health, 85*, 1237–1245.

Sedlak, A., & Broadhurst, D. (1996). *The third national incidence of child abuse and neglect: Final report.* National Center on Child Abuse and Neglect. Washington DC: U.S. Department of Health and Human Services.

Smith, L. (1994). The new welfare of illegitimacy. *Fortune,* 81–94.

Snell, T., & Morton, D. (1991). *Women in prison: Survey of prison inmates.* Bureau of Justice Statistics Special Report. Washington DC: U.S. Department of Justice.

Susin, L. (1999). *Issues in Prenatal Care Birth, 26*(3), 149–156.

Strauss, R. S. (1999). Influence of the home environment on the development of obesity in children. *Pediatrics, 103*(6), 85.

U.S. Census Bureau. (2002). *Children's living arrangements and characteristics.* Washington D.C.

U.S. Department of Health and Human Services. (1993). *Survey on child health.* National Center for Health Statistics. Washington, D.C.

Wassil-Grimm, C. (1994). *Where's Daddy? How divorced, single, and widowed mothers can provide what's missing when dad's missing.* New York, NY: Overlook Press.

Whitehead, B. (1995). Facing the challenges of fragmented families. *Philanthropy Roundtable, 9.1*, 21.

Zill, N., & Schoenborn, C. (1990). *Child development, learning, and emotional problems: Health of our nation's children.* National Center for Health Statistics. Washington DC: Department of Health and Human Services.

## ABOUT THE AUTHOR

K. T. Righter, aka K. Thomas, (RN, NC, and LMT) is best known for the award-winning book, *The Tao Te Ching De-Coded*. With a background in traditional and alternative therapies and counseling and with licensing in nursing, massage therapy and nutrition, Righter is passionate about promoting and delivering positive change to any person or any family. As a winner of various biology and academic awards, he strives to effect personal growth in an individual via interpersonal, physical, and mental health via research and application. Besides various health degrees, he also has a degree in criminal justice and considers his relationship with God and his four children—Isiah, Caroline, Kimberly, and Cheyenne—as his greatest treasures.

## WHY DAUGHTERS NEED THEIR DADS

Destined to be a groundbreaking book, in *Why Daughters Need Their Dads*, author K. T. Righter presents a holistic approach to the secrets that will help guide any woman to the greatness she deserves with his penetrating insight in this compelling and transforming book. Full of wise counsel and research, this book is a life-changer that will have a profound impact on any woman who wants to examine and change her life by giving her the power, confidence, and wisdom to succeed and finally create the life she has always desired. It also gives any dad the resources to put his daughter on the road to success and is a must-read for all those dads, daughters, and anyone else who wants to transform their lives and become who they finally want to be.

**KETNA PUBLISHING**: KETNA publishing is K. T. Righter and Erik Naugle. Erik is a true artiste, bringing a wide variety of formatting, graphic artistry, computer, and photographic skill and expertise to KETNA, which produces and adds visually smart and carefully detailed work to any project. Erik has worked in a variety of fields including photography and nursing and is an accomplished musician and an avid fisherman.

You can contact KETNA publishing at
kt123trailblazer@gmail.com or grobthom@aol.com.

www.ingramcontent.com/pod-product-compliance
Lightning Source LLC
Chambersburg PA
CBHW070613300426
44113CB00010B/1518